How to Land Your Dream Dental Associateship

The Educated Associate's Road Map to Success

Dr. Tony Schicktanz, DDS

How to Land Your Dream Dental Associateship: The Educated Associate's Road Map to Success

ISBN: 978-1-917327-39-8

First Edition

Acknowledgments

I would like to express my deep gratitude to several individuals who have played a significant role in the development of me as a man as well in the creation of this book. Their unwavering support, encouragement, and invaluable contributions have been instrumental in bringing this project to fruition.

First and foremost, I want to extend my heartfelt appreciation to my wife, Dr. Megan Schicktanz, for her steadfast belief in my abilities and her relentless support throughout this journey. Megan, your insightful ideas and meticulous editing have greatly enriched the manuscript, and I am grateful for your constant support of my often-crazy projects!

To my wonderful children, Riley and Leif, thank you for your patience and understanding during the countless hours I spent working on this book. I loved having the two of you on my lap while I composed the rough draft.

I would also like to express my deep gratitude to my parents, Mike and Wendy Schicktanz, for instilling in me the values of hard work, determination, and entrepreneurship. Your unyielding support and guidance have been essential in shaping my path, and I am grateful for the solid foundation you provided.

To my mother-in-law and father-in-law, Mark and Cathy Martinez, I extend my heartfelt thanks for your valuable contributions to this project. Your assistance with edits and your persistent encouragement along the way have been truly invaluable.

I would also like to acknowledge the countless other individuals who have played a crucial role in the development and completion of this book. Your support, feedback, and expertise have been imperative to the final product, and I extend my deepest appreciation to each and every one of you.

Finally, I would like to fep express my gratitude to the readers and supporters of me and this book. Your interest and enthusiasm have been a driving force behind its completion, and I am honored to have your support. If you found the information herein useful, please leave a review on my website, TheEducatedAssociate.com, so that I can help more dentists find their path. Additionally, my next big project will dig into financial education tailored to dentists. So be on lookout for that on the website as well.

Thank you all for being a part of this incredible journey and for helping to make this book a reality. And as always, stay drilling my friends!

Photograph by Kristina Graff photography

Contents

Disclaimer

This book and any associated content are intended for educational purposes only. They are not a substitute for professional advising services that may be required on a person to person basis.

Dr. Tony Schicktanz and The Educated Associate, LLC assume no responsibility or liability for adverse outcomes or damages that may result from the information provided. It is the sole responsibility of the reader to make their own informed choices and ensure compliance with medical, legal and ethical standards.

Introduction

How I Got Here

This book is the how-to guide I wish I had when I graduated dental school. Since graduating dental school in 2021, my passion project and my outlet has become the education of associate dentists and dental students. My interest in this niche was born from my own struggles to navigate the associate market shortly after graduating. Maybe you're here because you're going to start looking for your first associateship out of dental school. Maybe, like myself and many of my associate colleagues, you've already had an associate job, or two, or three, and you're tired of being burned by the system. Before I get into the tremendous amount of practical information and advice I've learned through my own research, and indeed, my own failings, let me first explain how this all started and what I hope you'll learn if you choose to use some of your very little free time reading these pages.

Sometime around the end of the fall semester of my DS4 year, I started looking for a job. Like a lot of other dentists, I've got a technical sort of approach to most tasks and tend to be on the more pragmatic side (maybe you can relate). I went looking for advice and guidance in the form of books, which didn't turn up any spectacular leads. Next, I turned to my professors and mentors. The problem with this approach was that most of them had either owned their own practice for the last one to three decades or had gone into academic dentistry and didn't have much timely wisdom to offer on the topic of navigating the ever-changing landscape of the associate dental market. By this time, I had already taken the obvious steps—had my neurotically detailed wife review and polish my CV, submitted a well-edited cover letter and CV to a few practices in my city of interest, reviewed job posting from Indeed.com. I had even received a few invitations to interview. This was great! "Maybe I don't need to be too technical about this. Afterall, everyone who graduates dental school in good standing ends up finding a job, and making decent money, right?" WRONG. So wrong, Tony. This was my first Learning Moment (LM). *Learning Moments are lessons incorporated throughout this book and there are a lot of them. These lessons are sometimes pitfalls to be avoided, while other times they are pointers I learned myself or from a colleague.*

It wasn't until I really started questioning my prospective employers and their recruiters that I realized I had a plethora of questions I needed to seriously consider before jumping into anything. Should I aim to work for a private practice? Should I even consider a DSO? I had heard so many horror stories that would make me think I should avoid it entirely, but some of these practices were offering things like signing bonuses and health insurance. Is it reasonable to expect a signing bonus? How negotiable is the salary for someone fresh out of dental school? What will be the difference in being paid on collection versus production? These were just the initial questions starting to form. Then the official contracts associated with the offers started to roll in. That's when I really began to feel like a monkey trying to solve a math problem. There was a lot of technical language in these multiple-page documents. I knew enough to know I shouldn't sign on the dotted line of a legal document without going through that baby line-by-line (yes, you absolutely need to do this with every contract you receive). But reading it carefully didn't necessarily equate to a meaningful understanding of the document. These contracts were asking for multiple years of legally and financially-binding commitment from me.

I thought, "Surely, this warrants spending some money on an attorney, right?" So, I went about researching how much it would cost me to have an attorney review my contract(s). Keep in mind, at this time, I was still a dental student (so poor) and my wife was a resident physician (so making very little money) living in another city, and we had a small child whose daycare costs more than our rent and groceries combined (no joke). Maybe you, too, are a dental student trying to figure out how on earth you're going to afford an attorney's fees. Maybe you can subside on Ramen noodles and pick up a side gig rather than sleeping? Just kidding. Don't do that. You, my friend, are the reason I wrote this book! I *know* that not everyone looking for an associateship can afford the thousands of dollars it would take to have an attorney review multiple contracts. I also personally know associates who have paid the hefty sum to have their contract green lighted by an attorney only to realize they themselves did not truly understand what they had agreed to and were trapped in a bad situation. Fun fact—just because someone is a contract lawyer or offers the service of contract review doesn't necessarily mean they understand the nuance of dental associate pay structure, how a dental office functions, or the many factors that might make a job more or less appealing to an associate.

I wrote this book so I could answer the many questions you have while trying to find an ideal associateship *for you specifically.* I wrote this book because I've seen some of the most brilliant dentists, I've worked with get trapped in jobs they hate. Since starting my online platform, I've spent hundreds of hours talking to associates from all over the country about their jobs and reviewing their contracts. Here's what I can tell you: the bad offers are out there. And they're sneaky. They whisper sweet nothings in your weary ears and then tie financial handcuffs around your wrists for multiple years. But here's the good news: the amazing offers, the dream jobs, the perfect fits—those are out there, too! You just need an approach to finding and securing them.

This book is written so that, if it so suits you, you can skip chapters and refer only to those that interest or will serve you. I know your time is precious. But if you take nothing else from this book, remember these three points so that you will be more likely to find the job that serves you:

1) One dentist's perfect dream associateship is another dentist's hell on earth. You need to know yourself, first and foremost. Reading this book will help you reflect on the many aspects of your personality, financial, clinical, and personal goals that alter what the ideal job situation will look like for you.
2) I don't care who you are, you must understand the contract you are signing. Not your dad, your spouse, or your attorney. YOU. And I will go through the technical language and pay structure types to help you with this. I'm sick and tired of seeing dentists who can absolutely ball on their clinical and surgical skills work jobs that make them miserable because they didn't understand contract language.
3) You matriculated to dental school and graduated. You have undoubtedly overcome a great deal and sacrificed a lot of time and sleep to become an extremely valuable workforce commodity. Do not sell yourself short. Find the job you want.

As much as I love pontificating about associateships, I need to wrap this introduction up. Let me leave you with this story and some parting thoughts. I currently work at a job I love. It's a two-associate, corporate-owned spot in Tempe, AZ. My co-associate, Dr. Fred Wood (a dental baller if ever there was one), is a 78-year-old man who has been practicing dentistry for 40+ years. He has been an associate and an owner and has endless wisdom to impart. He told me that, when he graduated dental school 40 years ago, his very first job offer was $150K per year for three days per week. In contrast, my first associate offer (before I had gained the knowledge I share in this book), was $140K per year, working 5 days per week, and really ended up being 50-60 hours per week of my time. I was given no signing bonus. I stumbled, tripped, and fell ass backwards so that you can skip and run. Don't sleep on this opportunity.

Sadly, as you are likely already aware, dentists are being compensated less and less on the average. Adding insult to injury is the disgusting rise in the cost of our education, and therefore, likely, your student loans. We can debate the root cause of this, but certainly one contributing factor is the rise is DSOs and the increasing difficulty of owning a successful private practice when competing with the large DSOs. But dentists are not fools. We know that this service, this industry, it does not exist without US. I wrote this book to hopefully play some small role in forcing a change in the dental market. When we as a collective group of professionals empower ourselves with the knowledge of contract terminology and pay structure as well as the skills of excellent negotiators, we push the market toward offering better contracts to dentists as a whole. Better dentists, who are not overworked, underpaid, or toiling away in a toxic work environment provide better patient care. Let us arm ourselves with the knowledge and skill required to negotiate the contracts we want from the jobs we've dreamed of so that we can provide patients with the dental care that is so important to their overall health. And as always, stay drilling my friends.

Chapter 1

Where to Start: Targeting Your Search—Key Elements of an Associateship

A career in dentistry can be very rewarding in countless ways if you select the correct associateship. Conversely, working in the wrong associateship may bring on burnout, apprehension, and anxiety. Before you begin your search, I recommend you acquaint yourself with the key elements of an associateship: mentorship, the type of procedures you hope to perform, patient population, location, owner type, and, if possible, the culture of the practice.

Almost every student doctor I talk to puts mentorship at the top of their wish list. My follow-up question is "What specific things do you expect from the mentorship?" Some doctors want to use the first year or two to hone their clinical skills in order to become efficient in bread-and-butter dentistry and build a profitable practice. These goals call for a particular kind of mentorship. The student who wants to learn more about running the business, however, will be looking for a very different kind. This is a key point. I worked for a practice owner who was incredibly willing to help me with anything clinical. She would stop whatever she was doing whenever I asked for help and show me, for example, a trick to remove an impacted molar. On the other hand, she was very reluctant to give up information about the business end of the practice.

Since, at that point in my career, I was looking for clinical guidance and signed on knowing that's what I'd be getting, I felt I'd made the right decision. If, however, I had been interested in a mentorship focusing on practice management, I would have been deeply disappointed. The secret to learning what you want comes down to asking the correct question. The question in this case is "What kind of mentorship do I really want?" I suggest that you write down precisely what you want to learn as well as what will be required to accomplish those objectives. Create an avatar of the mentor of your dreams and compare it to the owners you have a chance to work with. Be very honest with yourself and the owners during the interview process since you want to start this relationship out on the right foot.

<u>My Example Coming Out of Dental School</u>

> <u>What I want to learn:</u> Quadrant dentistry, placing implants, and doing molar root canals.

> <u>Avatar:</u> A mentor with at least five years of clinical experience since graduating from dental school or residency. The mentor needs to be doing quadrant dentistry daily, placing implants regularly, and be able to complete molar root canals.

> <u>Discovery:</u> I used the dental office website to see what types of procedures were commonly performed, and then I followed up with patient reviews to get a basic understanding of what had recently been done in the office.

As you go further into the interview process, you can simply ask about the kind of mentorship offered. More on this later.

A second element to consider is the procedure that best meshes with who you are as a dental provider. Some of us are aesthetic dentists, and doing anterior composite veneers gets our juices going, while others can't stand the idea of crowning a tooth and instead go with implants for tooth replacements. If a cosmetic dentist ended up in a practice doing primarily extractions and implants for denture rehabilitations, it's not likely they'd ever fully be satisfied in their career no matter how much money they earned or how many patients they treated. The same is true for the implant dentist who is doing anterior resins day in and day out. They would soon feel the fatigue of burnout.

This is why deciding what you like and are good at doing is important. Now, I'm not saying you should avoid things you're not good at. For example, I was really bad at molar root canals coming out of dental school. I chose a practice with a doctor who did one molar or so a week. I knew I didn't want molar endos on my schedule every day, but a few a month would allow me to expand my skill set. In other words, I suggest finding a sweet spot where the office does mostly the stuff you like doing while mixing in a little of everything else so you can sharpen your clinical acumen in various surgical specialties. Again, write down the procedures you want to do. Write down the procedures you are not willing to do. Write down the procedures where you need improvement. To assess what procedures are commonly performed at an office, use the dental practice website. Also, talk to the staff while there interviewing. The primary doctor likely talks about their normal day with you during the interview, so use all the information available to gain a better understanding of the office's typical procedure mixture.

<u>My Example Coming Out of Dental School</u>

- ➢ <u>Procedures I want to do and am capable of doing now:</u> Extractions, crown and bridge, direct restorative, anterior RCTs, and removable prosthodontics.

- ➢ <u>Procedures I do NOT want to do:</u> Aesthetic rehabilitations, full-mouth rehabilitations, and periodontal therapies.

- ➢ <u>Procedures I want to improve on (mentorship):</u> Quadrant dentistry, implant placement, and molar RCTs.

Another important consideration is the patient population the practice serves. Do you wake up energized to help the underserved? Or do you want to see 2–6 patients each day in a biomimetic-dentistry setting? Those are important questions to ask yourself because you'll be spending countless hours away from your family and friends, dealing primarily with patients each day. If every single hour you're away from home seems like you're watching the clock, then you may not have picked the right patient population to serve (LM). At the end of the day, helping people should feel rewarding to you. I personally have found that serving the right demographic weighs heavily on how rewarded (or not) I feel as a dentist.

Use your dental school rotations and any pre-dental schoolwork experience in healthcare as guides to help you make this decision. Additionally, the worksheet below will help you choose which patient type may be best suited to you.

<u>Finding Your Niche: Key Questions to Consider When Determining Your Ideal Patient Population:</u>

1. Are you interested in treating patients with specific dental conditions or needs?
2. Do you prefer preventive care or restorative therapies?
3. Do you prefer to work with patients who require routine dental care or more complex procedures?
4. Are you willing to work on patients with specific dental phobias or anxieties?
5. Do you want to work with patients who have special needs?
6. What is the age range you tend to work best with?
7. Is there a specific demographic you aim to treat? Athletes/famous people?
8. Are you interested in providing cosmetic dental care?

9. Do you prefer to work with patients who need long-term care or patients who only come in for occasional dental care?
10. Do you want to work at a practice that cares for a specific community, such as low-income or underserved populations?

The three buzzwords you'll hear in real estate are *location, location, location.* Similarly, the location of the dental office or offices where you'll be working is often critical. Again, you'll likely be working long hours away from your family and friends, doing what can be an emotionally, mentally, and physically challenging job. In one of my first positions, I was commuting 20–30 minutes to and from work. I was working at an office open from 7:30 a.m. until 5:00 p.m. This meant that I was on the road or at work from at least 7:00 a.m. until 6:00 p.m. Monday through Friday. If you tally that up, I was essentially working 50–60 hours a week (LM).

One way to cut down on hours away from home is to arrange for a short commute. I once had a colleague who literally lived a 2-minute walk away from the office. He'd go home at lunch, heat up fresh food in the comfort of his own kitchen, and even catch a 20-minute power nap each day. While I was usually stuck eating in the office kitchen by myself or sitting in traffic after work, he was already on his couch with a snack. So, avoid commutes if at all possible, especially early in your career.

Another side note on location: Pay very close attention to practices that have more than one site. I'd worked my way through an entire interview process and was shown one office, but on my contract there was a separate office site listed (it was even under a different name). Upon investigation I discovered that the owner actually had three totally separate private practices. He showed me around the office in the city, which was near where I lived. He tried to convince me that I'd be at this office and never even mentioned his other office(s), which, even on a sunny day, was a 30-minute commute into the mountains. This was an instant deal-breaker for me. First of all, I felt lied to. Second, I had no intention of working in the mountains while living in the city. I was literally about to sign this contract when I noticed this subtle difference. To avoid making such mistakes, I suggest running multiple versions of negotiated contracts through editing software to check for any changes, no matter how small.

A final note on location. Rural settings often offer the highest earnings and low cost of living. There's a job search strategy called Geographic Arbitrage where healthcare providers select for work in these rural areas due to the reasons above. On the other hand, these jobs tend to also offer the least support—by a long shot. I had a friend who landed his first associateship in a very rural setting; I mean no other dentists for over 100 miles. My friend was making money hand over fist but quit after six months. He hadn't been seeing an absurd number of patients, nor were the patients overly complex. And they all paid in cash. But he had no one to whom he could turn to ask questions, no one to ask for help in the middle of a hard case, and he felt pressured by the patients to provide *all* treatments so they "wouldn't have to drive to the city." This burned him more times than he could count. Maybe one day he'll be ready to live in the middle of nowhere and cover all forms of dentistry, but taking this position immediately out of dental school, he now admits, was a mistake. In light of my friend's experience, I recommend a location where there's a peer you can at least talk to and specialists to whom you can refer patients when really needed.

The two final considerations you should take into account before starting the job search are less tangible than those we've already covered. Moreover, they are likely to be difficult to figure out based solely on studying a practice's website, so you will probably have to rely on your interviews/in-person exchanges. That said, any insight you can gain before the interview process starts can be of tremendous value.

First and foremost, you need to decide what type of authority figure you work best with. If you know that you don't do well with someone looking over your shoulder, watching every step you make, you need to find an owner who believes in autonomy of care. Asking questions about autonomy can shed a lot of light on how closely the owner plans to monitor you.

Another aspect of the owner-associate relationship I've found to be of the utmost importance is how well the two of you communicate. You are likely to be in close physical proximity to the owner. Some owners, however, have multiple locations, so communication may be remote as well. However, you and the owner keep in contact, having similar communicative skills will make the relationship much easier. The best way to test how well you two communicate is the interview process, along with how they treat you when they show you their office. If you feel talked down to, the job probably isn't right for you, so it's much better to know that *before* negotiating the contract.

The final element to review is the practice culture. Again, this is something you'll discern more readily on your tour of the office/during interviews, but again, anything you can learn before interviewing can be worth its weight in gold. Go to the practice website. Try to get an idea of office turnover for both clinical and non-clinical positions. If there's a new assistant or front-desk worker every month, there's probably something going on there that calls for a closer look. Go to Google. Check the office reviews. Does the office manager or owner respond to negative reviews? If so, do they accept criticism and try to resolve the issue, or are they combative? Owners or offices with a lot of negative reviews, especially recent ones, are suspect. If the owner is combative over negative reviews, run the other way! ▶

Side note, ▶, red flags, will show up periodically throughout the text like the Learning Moments. They are used to draw your attention to a particular problem or issue that could be important to you. In chapter 13, you will find a summary of all the Red Flags from throughout the book.

Lastly, if you live in the city or have friends or relatives in the city where the office is, you can ask for grassroots information about the practice. This information is very likely to be biased but could be of tremendous value. A colleague and friend once told me a cautionary tale about interviewing for a job at a specialist's office. The owner already had an associate working for him. According to my colleague, the associate was basically her doppelgänger. As she put it, "We were both young, blond females." To her surprise, my colleague found out that the owner and his associate were in a somewhat ambiguous romantic relationship.

My friend used her ties in the community to dig more deeply. She learned that the owner had been married for some 15 years and gotten divorced just a year earlier. During the divorce he'd taken up with a young doctor in training—his current associate. The owner had more or less coerced her into specialist training and then into his office by keeping up a romantic relationship with her. My friend decided very quickly that she wouldn't be working for this dentist. By looking into things about the practice that seemed fishy to her on a gut level, she may have saved herself years of harassment, unhappiness, and feeling trapped. Be sure to trust your gut when working through the interview process (LM).

Next, I will continue to ask you to truly explore yourself so we can ensure you find the associateship of your dreams now and once you're working there. We will tackle one of the most challenging questions in all of associateship: to DSO or not to DSO? We will discuss the major similarities and differences between private practice, Dental Service Organizations (DSOs), and nonprofits.

Chapter Summary Points:

1. **Audit yourself on the following topics related to associate dentistry to make sure the practice is similar to what you are actually seeking.**
   a. **Mentorship – type, degree of help, and for how long**

   b. **Types of procedures provided in the office**

   c. **Patient population/demographics**

   d. **Location/proximity to your residence**

   e. **Owner type – communication style**

   f. **Office culture**

Chapter 2

Private Practice vs. DSO vs. Nonprofit – What's Best for You?

Overview

When I came out of dental school, I had no experience working in a dental office. I'd done about 50 hours of shadowing in various clinics, but I was as green as they come in terms of how an office is run. Additionally, most of my clinical education in dental school fell during the initial COVID shutdowns of 2020. Therefore, my experience with clinical rotations wasn't as thorough as I would have liked. Most students who graduated from CU before me were able to do several rotations in various practice types, including private practice, corporate dental care, and even nonprofit organizations, such as Denver Health. These are the same job choices offered to the vast majority of graduating students not seeking residency training or military duty. If you're like me, you had no real understanding of the differences among the above organizations. A brief overview is therefore in order.

Private Practice:

➢ In a private practice, a dentist usually owns the practice and has complete control over how it's run. In some states a hygienist or other staff member can also own.

➢ The owner is responsible for all aspects of the business, including finances, marketing, hiring staff, and managing patient care.

- ➢ The owner has the potential to earn a higher income than in other settings, but also has more financial risk.

  - ▪ Some offices claim net earnings of ~50% of their overall revenue.

- ➢ An associate dentist in a private practice may have more autonomy and a closer relationship with patients.

  - ▪ Private practices often have smaller staffs and offer more personal ties to employees.

  - ▪ In my experience, if you maintain a good working relationship with the owner, they'll usually do what you ask. For example, I asked an owner to buy a different type of composite for my use, and he had no problem with that. In a DSO practice, the business is so large that they've likely struck a deal with a composite manufacturer, and that's the composite you'll be using at that office.

<u>DSO (Dental Service Organization)</u>: Think Corporate

- ➢ DSO is a company that provides management and administrative services to dental practices, which may be owned by the DSO or by individual dentists. This is a key distinction. I've interviewed at DSO-owned and DSO-managed practices. I have now worked at a DSO-managed practice too. They have a very different feel from privately owned practices.
  - ▪ While this feeling is not universal, most DSOs are staffed by people who haven't worked in dentistry. These people may not be accustomed to nuances of dentistry, but they have likely had success somewhere else in business. Maybe they ran a successful medical spa. These people come in and try and influence the business operations of the dental office. Some changes are certainly for the better, while an equal number are

likely for the worse. If you have been there for one of these transition periods of a practice acquisition by a DSO, you know what I am talking about. Again, it's not all bad or all good. It's just a more business-oriented approach that feels different.

➢ The DSO handles tasks such as billing, marketing, and hiring, while the dentists focus on patient care.

- In some cases there will be more pressure on the dentist to produce than before.

➢ DSOs may provide opportunities for career growth and continuing education as well as access to resources and support.

- My experience has been that obtaining job offers at DSOs as a new graduate may be easier than finding that one private practice left in the neighborhood.

➢ The oft-cited advantage of working at a DSO is increased time for patient care and in some settings a multidisciplinary setup with many dental specialties in-house to help with your learning.

➢ An associate dentist in a DSO may have less control over the practice and less autonomy in decision-making.

<u>Nonprofit Dental Clinic:</u>

➢ A nonprofit dental clinic is typically operated by a charitable organization or government agency.

➢ The clinic may provide services to underserved populations, such as low-income families or those without insurance.

➢ The focus is on providing affordable care rather than generating profits.

- ➢ The pay for an associate dentist in a nonprofit is often lower when compared to a private practice or DSO.

  - There is a higher likelihood of a salary as opposed to a production/ collections-based compensation structure, however.

- ➢ Many nonprofits offer excellent student-loan repayment options and less stressful work environments for associates.

- ➢ Generally, nonprofit dental organizations that meet certain criteria can apply for tax-exempt status under Section 501(c)(3) of the Internal Revenue Code.

  - This means that the organization is exempt from paying federal income tax on its earnings, and donations to the organization are tax-deductible for the donors.

  - To qualify for tax-exempt status, a nonprofit dental organization must meet certain requirements, including the following:

    - ➢ Being organized and operated exclusively for charitable, educational, religious, or scientific purposes.

    - ➢ Not engaging in political activities or lobbying.

    - ➢ Not distributing earnings to individuals or shareholders.

    - ➢ Limiting the amount of private benefit that individuals can receive from the organization.

Nonprofit dental organizations that do not qualify for tax-exempt status under Section 501(c)(3) may be able to apply for other types of tax exemption, such as under Section 501(c)(4) or 501(c)(6). These types of organizations may have different tax obligations and limitations on their activities, so it's important to consult with a tax professional to determine the best tax status for a nonprofit dental organization.

<u>To Corporation or Not to Corporation: A Decision Tree for Choosing Between Corporate (DSO) and Private Practice Dentistry:</u>

<u>Financials:</u>

According to data from the Bureau of Labor and Statistics (BLS), as of May 2020 there were 111,400 dentists employed in the U.S. The article mentioned, however, that many self-employed, private practice owners may not have been included in this data. The American Dental Association (ADA) therefore estimated there were some 200,419 working dentists in 2020, although they expect that number to decline to around 196,000 by the next decade.

Generally speaking, the ADA estimates that between 2,000 and 2,500 dentists will retire annually over the span of the next decade. The ADA cites the high degree of retiring dentists and decreased enrollments in dental school nationally as the reason for the overall decline in the next decade.

As of 2021 there were 66 CODA-accredited dental schools in the U.S., and the ADA estimated there were a total of 5,596 dental school graduates in that same year. The BLS lists the average wage earned by a dentist in the U.S. in 2020 as $164,010. According to the *DentalPost Annual Report for 2020*, the average wage of an associate at a DSO-style practice was slightly higher: $166,000. It's worth noting, however, that this figure is unlikely to reflect the income of all dentists working in DSOs and was a mixture of generalists and specialists, which can account for significant differences in pay. The BLS estimates that private practice associates earned an average of $167,650 in 2020 (again, slightly higher). There was very little data differentiating pay between DSO-owned and DSO-managed operations. Compensation is noticeably lower in the nonprofit sector. Data from the website Payscale cites an average annual salary of just $103,000, although the fact that many nonprofit dentists may receive other benefits, such as loan forgiveness, should be taken into consideration.

Highest Average Earnings = Private Practice > DSO Practice > > > Nonprofit

The number of (<,>) noted in the diagram depicts the degree of difference between practice types.

<u>Work-Life Balance:</u>

Less reliable than data on earnings is the data on work-life balance. I'll review data on average hours worked, average number of patients seen, and overall provider satisfaction to provide some benchmark numbers for comparisons. Full disclosure: Most of this data is survey-based, so its reliability is questionable, but it's the best we've got, and since we practice evidence-based dentistry we might as well base our career review on evidence.

According to a 2019 survey by the ADA, a private practice dentist in the U.S. works an average of 36.1 hours a week. In 2020 *DentalPost* estimated a general dentist would average 32.9 hours per week in a DSO-style practice. A study by the National Network for Oral Health Access (NNOHA) showed that full-time dentists in nonprofits work the 36-40 hours of a typical weekly schedule. The same ADA survey from 2019 estimated that a general dentist working in a private practice would see 72.6 patients per work week (14.5 patients per day). The *DentalPost* survey from 2020 estimates 70.4 patients seen per week by a general dentist working at a DSO practice (14.1 patients per day). An NNOHA survey estimates that a single dentist at a nonprofit sees an average of 12–16 patients a day. According to the ADA survey, 78% of dentists working in private practice in 2020 reported being either very satisfied or somewhat satisfied with their current jobs; however, I would expect some significant changes in the satisfaction of providers in the post-pandemic world. The same survey suggests that nearly the same percentage of dentists working in DSO practice (77%) expressed similar levels of job satisfaction. The NNOHA survey reported that more than 80% of dentists working in nonprofits fell into this job-satisfaction category.

If you look at each of those variables individually or try and draw a composite picture from them it's hard to make exact inferences. This is one area you will have to decide for yourself: Do I prefer shorter hours or fewer patients? How much weight do I give to the 1%–3% differences in provider satisfaction nationally in a pre-pandemic world? It is truly a toss-up and could go either way.

Hours worked/week = DSO Practice > Private Practice > Nonprofit

Number of patients seen/week = DSO Practice > Private Practice > Nonprofit

Provider satisfaction = Nonprofit > Private Practice > DSO

<u>Patient Demographics and Technology/ Equipment in the Office:</u>

Other important aspects that can be compared across office types include the patient base and equipment/technology. Most DSOs serve a specific patient population, which can vary based on the organization's mission and priorities. Some focus on children or the elderly, while others confine themselves to the underserved. A report from the National Association of Dental Plans stated that DSOs tend to serve a higher number of Medicaid patients. A dental practice survey conducted in 2019 by the ADA found that private practice dentists treated patients between the ages of 21 and 64, most of whom had dental insurance, about 47% of the time. Dentists in nonprofits treat almost exclusively underserved or Medicaid patient populations.

In terms of technology, the largest difference lies between nonprofits and the other two groups. One of my dental school friends is a nonprofit dentist. The office he works in has one digital X-ray machine and no ability to take a panoramic or CBCT. If you're wondering, "Does he really take analog radiographs as a dentist practicing in 2024?" the answer is *yes*. If you work in the nonprofit sector, it's unlikely that you'll get to use much if any modern technologies as they are released into the market. So, if technology is the thing that gets your juices flowing in the morning, you can probably rule out nonprofits from the start.

On the other hand, DSO and private practice offices, offer excellent technology options. Generally speaking, DSOs seem to offer a slight advantage in their ability to invest in new technologies and then rapidly implement them across multiple locations. The larger size of the DSOs allows them to have centralized resources and procurement processes, which in turn allow for the most cost-effective purchase of these technologies. That said, the most advanced office I've ever seen is a private practice. So, based on my own experience, I'd say you can't rely on the average case to know whether a DSO or private practice will offer more advanced technology; it really depends on the specific practice. All in all, the level of technology found in the average DSO or private practice is likely very comparable but certainly more advanced than that of a nonprofit.

Technology Advancements = Private Practice = DSO >>> Nonprofit

After finishing Chapter 2, you should feel more confident when deciding if a DSO, private practice, or nonprofit is right for you. There is no single right decision. I have now worked in two private practices and one DSO-style practice. They have all been great in some regards and not so great in others. My experience is well summarized in the graphics above, and I would personally agree with most of the data from the studies included in the discussion.

At the end of the day, finding the right people within the office where I worked has proven more valuable than knowing if the place was a private or DSO office (LM). If you can get along with the other dentists, office manager, and the person who will be doing most of your assisting, then that office could be amazing despite being in a setting you maybe didn't think you would like. That was my experience with a DSO. I never wanted to work in a corporate setting, but after interviewing twice and going out to dinner with the other dentist there, I was hooked. In retrospect I have enjoyed the DSO and private offices individually for separate reasons, but all three places overall have been great because the people working there with me were great. Select for people you get along with, and your daily work will be more enjoyable.

Next, we will delve into where to target your search. We will start by discussing leveraging the in-person relationships you created before or during dental school; if that wasn't you, it's not a big deal, as we will also discuss how to leverage online media to target the job of your dreams.

Chapter Summary Points:

1. **Realize the similarities and differences among private practices, DSOs, and nonprofits**

2. **Greatest earnings = private practice > DSO >>> nonprofit**

3. **Weekly hours = DSO > private practice > nonprofit**

4. **Number of patients seen each week = DSO > private practice > nonprofit**

5. **Provider satisfaction = nonprofit > private practice > DSO**

6. **Technology available = private practice = DSO >>> nonprofit**

Chapter 3

Navigating Your Path and Finding Opportunities

The best way to start your search is by speaking with someone in the dental field who has firsthand knowledge of the specific geographic radius within which you'd like to work. The size of the radius should take into consideration rural vs. city options. If you choose a large city, pinpoint where specifically you'd like to work in that city. Obviously, you could try a local dentist, especially the owner of a practice. Owners tend to be very well connected and would likely know whether there are any openings in the area. Additionally, they can give you their opinion on "that other practice." Key words to keep in mind: "their opinion." Be sure to take bias into account and make your own judgments.

If you're smarter than I was, you did some networking in dental school. Do you remember that Patterson sales representative you spoke to for over an hour at the dental convention? Well, they know all the dentists in your area. They also know where the best offices are located. They may not be able to get you a foot in the door, but they can sure point you in the right direction. If you're reading this as a first-to-third-year dental student, you're way ahead of the game, and you should start networking at dental conventions or when presenters visit your school. Taking the small step of introducing yourself to the representative could result in them eventually pointing you to the office of your dreams.

If, like me, you don't have a friend or family member in the dental field, you're not out of luck. This book was written to help you through this challenging process, and you'll be amazed that *your* first job will better match your dreams than your friend's first job, despite the fact that upon graduation they're going to work in their dad's office.

There are many options on the Web. The vast majority of students with whom I graduated or with whom I've spoken since my graduation were in the same situation (no friends or family in the dental field). We all turned to the Web to get a toehold. The obvious places to start are the large job platforms like Indeed or Glassdoor. In fact, this is a strategy I've used a number of times to land the job I was looking for. This is why in the next section we'll discuss writing a résumé that gets you through the AI software websites use to analyze and, often, screen out résumés.

I think of this strategy as my "résumé funnel." To illustrate, we'll use a simple résumé. Its simplicity will ensure that it's "readable" by AI software and that it takes this vital first step on large web pages. Many résumés that were made to "stand out," on the other hand, just confuse AI software, and a potentially great applicant becomes dead in the water. I'll show you how to avoid this frustrating and costly mistake. You can think of getting past the scanning AI as getting your primary dental school application passed along for a secondary review. Now you'll be dealing with the human beings involved in the business.

Side note on using these large web pages: The résumé you submit will become "free game" for anyone on the Internet. I still get random emails asking me to interview for a job. Furthermore, sometimes the jobs offered aren't in dentistry or my designated geographic region. For example, I've been asked to interview for a veterinary job in San Francisco although I've never worked with animals and never looked for work in California. So be ready to deal with spam emails or phone calls down the road.

Also, healthcare recruiters are smart. They sift these web pages to find the résumés of applicants who want to work in their region. These recruiters are more like "sports agents"—they show up around contract time, do their best to push the deal along, collect a large paycheck, and never speak with you again.

A friend of mine in dental school was approached by a recruiter based in the medium-size city where he was planning to work. The city was in desperate need of dentists. Several offices had most likely hired the recruiter to find them an associate. The recruiter saw my friend's résumé on Indeed and reached out to him. The recruiter, who seemed like a really nice guy, asked my friend whether he could "use" my friend's résumé to help him find a job. There would be no charge to him even if the recruiter found my friend his "dream job." This seemed like a win-win. My friend, however, never signed an agreement with the recruiter. He simply allowed him to use his résumé. Within a few days my friend had several offices reaching out to him. He was very excited. It seemed the recruiter was doing exactly what he'd promised.

Flash forward a month and my friend was in the midst of negotiating a contract with an office he really liked. During negotiations, however, it quickly became obvious that the office would be unable to provide my friend any benefits whatsoever. Additionally, the pay for the area was low, no relocation or signing bonus was forthcoming, and the office made no real attempt to change the initial contract. My friend then reached out to a banker who was familiar with how recruiting works. The banker explained that the office likely had to pay the recruiter around 20% of his anticipated first-year salary once the contract was signed. So, the recruiter was probably getting a check for $20,000-$40,000 once the deal closed. No wonder there was no financial wiggle room in the contract! My friend was such a good match for the office he ended up taking the deal despite the lack of financial incentive in the contract.

At the end of the day, he indirectly paid the recruiter roughly $30,000 by letting him use his résumé when, according to my friend, he'd have likely found this office on his own. So only let someone use your résumé or seek out a recruiter as a last resort. In the long run, it'll cost you much more than you think. If you follow my advice, you should never need a recruiter, which means that, by reading this short book, you may be saving/ making yourself thousands of dollars. If you still have an issue finding an associateship after reading this book and applying the principles, please reach out to me on my website, TheEducatedAssociate.com and set up a free 15-minute consultation with yours truly to see if I can help you land the job you are looking for.

Another great place to start your search is Facebook (groups) or other social media. One Facebook group I've seen used successfully is Dental Practice Matchmaker. At the time of this writing, they had more than 13,000 member dentists and dental practice owners. They don't allow sales or solicitation, so it's a good place to get some geographically sorted leads. Owners list their practices when they're in need of an associate or they're trying to sell their practice. Potential associates can also list their credentials and their preferred locations. It really is like a matchmaking page for dental jobs. An excellent tool to connect directly with owners, it's best suited to individuals looking to work in a private practice.

I've also seen dentists talk about needing an associate on their practice Instagram/Facebook page or even on their personal Instagram or Facebook pages.

Don't forget to keep your social media profiles professional or in private mode to ensure that you have as many job options as possible. Moreover, if you're attempting to be an influencer, be sure your message isn't insensitive. You never know nowadays what someone will find offensive, and you don't want to put off a possible employer.

Speaking from my own experience, I've had many offices/practice owners reach out to me via social media to inquire about hiring me. I even had someone offer me an associate job through

Instagram without an interview—I literally received a contract through Instagram messages! If you develop a dental personality on social media, this could be a reality for you as well. If you haven't yet checked out my social media accounts, please use the QR codes below and follow me for more free and actionable advice!

Additionally, there are many great websites that help with associate dentist placement such as DentalPost, DentalJobs.net, and Dental Headhunters. Briefly, DentalPost is a job board and career resource specifically for dental professionals, connecting job seekers with dental practices looking to hire. It helps dentists, dental hygienists, dental assistants, and other dental professionals find job opportunities in the dental industry. It is free for job seekers, but the hiring offices pay a fee. DentalJobs.net is a website that serves as a job board for dental professionals. It is a platform where dental professionals can search for job opportunities and apply for positions in the dental field. This website has both a free and a boosted feature, which costs around $25 at the time of this writing for job seekers.

My last online place to look is good old Craigslist. Be wary, but I've heard some colleagues mention they had luck on Craigslist after dental school.

The final thing to discuss regarding an online job search is headhunters. A headhunter, also known as an executive recruiter or search consultant, is a professional who specializes in finding and recruiting candidates for job positions, in our case, of course, dentists for companies/offices. I brought up a headhunter earlier in this chapter when discussing my friend. They often work on behalf of employers to identify and attract top talent for specific roles. They get paid when they get a dentist on-contract with the employer who hired them. The key word there is that they get paid AFTER a dentist is on-contract. So they will work tirelessly to close a deal and then disappear into the night with a bag of cash, never to been seen or heard from again. They typically earn a commission, which is often a percentage of the yearly compensation of the dentist they sign—for example, 15% of the dentist's anticipated earnings. This is often in the neighborhood of $15,000-$40,000, depending on the specific job and the location. Once they sign an associate to an office, they get a check for $20,000-ish in most cases.

I want to warn you of headhunters and encourage you to allow them access to your résumé, CV, cover letter, or anything about you on a very rare basis. I have seen these headhunters work online by trolling job websites. These recruiters are smart. They often look innocent on these job websites and approach job seekers with comments like "If you let me use your résumé, I can help you find a job in the area you are hoping to work, and it won't cost you a dime, even if I find you the job you want." Wow, that sure sounds like an amazing person! They want to help me for free—that's cool. Things that sound too good to be true often are! Be wary of this behavior online as very often free things come with a hidden cost. In the headhunter case, it can come out of your possible signing or relocation bonus, or make for fewer benefits or lower pay, as the office must compensate for the large check they had to write the recruiter upon your signing. When you "let" the headhunter use your résumé, you gave them permission to find you an office, and if they do, they get paid by the office and it comes out of your future earnings. Use these recruiters as a last step only!

So far, we have looked at the online search from our perspective, as an associate. I think it is also worthwhile to view it from the owners' standpoint. Many private practice owners are wearing many hats, which makes sense because they are dentists, entrepreneurs, in charge of hiring and firing, and much more. They are also compensated for their success in those many areas by owning a practice. Personally, I think it is a red flag for an owner to tell you that they "expect you to wear many hats" in the online job description or in any portion of an interview ▶. You are there to be an associate dentist, and unless your agreement is compensating you for doing more than dentistry, I'd run away from an owner telling you that you will be expected to do more than dentistry by signing there. Another red flag I've seen in job descriptions is "We're family." While we all want to work in a nice work setting, the family vibe is often not for work, and moreover these offices often have a toxic work culture they want to hide with a rosy statement like "We're family." It could also mean you will be invited to many non-work-related events that aren't mandatory but will feel very mandatory whenever you miss one ▶.

At the end of the chapter, we now have a plan for how to start our search. Maybe you already know someone in the dental community; that's an obvious place to start, but realize you will be getting a biased opinion. If you were better than I was, you did some networking in dental school and can now leverage those relationships with Patterson or Henry Schein representatives and see if they can get you in the door somewhere. If you were like me or aren't having luck leveraging a personal relationship, then do what most millennials prefer anyway (by the way, I am a millennial) and go online. Consider starting with a large website like Glassdoor or Indeed or smaller, more dental-specific groups like the Facebook group Dental Practice Matchmaker. As a last resort consider using good old Craigslist. Remember to watch out for red flags like "we're family" or we expect you to "wear many hats," as these might be clues to a problem within a practice.

Chapter Summary Points:

1. **Leverage personal relationships in the dental community in which you plan to work**

2. **If you haven't graduated dental school, start networking with representatives like those from Henry Schein or Patterson**

    a. **If you did this in school, use those representatives to see if they can get you in the door somewhere**

3. **Go online**

    a. **Large websites – Glassdoor or Indeed**

    b. **Smaller, more dental-specific – Dental Practice Matchmaker on Facebook**

    c. **Be wary of headhunters**

4. **Craigslist**

5. **Job description red flags**

    a. **"We're family"**

    b. **"We expect you to wear many hats"**

Chapter 4

Preparing Your Materials – The "Resume Funnel"

<u>Preparing Your Résumé/CV and Cover Letters: the "Résumé Funnel":</u>

When I first work with graduating dentists who have made it through Chapters 1 through chapter 3 and understand how to target their search, I often get this question next: "Should I prepare a résumé or a curriculum vitae [CV]?" The answer to this question lies, again, in the details. There's a subtle distinction between a CV and a résumé, which will become very important when you actually apply for a position in a particular office.

In short, a résumé is a one- or two-page document that lists your education, work experience, skills, and any achievements in chronological order. It's often tailored to the specific job and used for most job applications in the United States. A CV, on the other hand, is a much more detailed document that provides a comprehensive overview of academic and professional backgrounds, publications, presentations, and research. It's often longer and is commonly used for most job applications in the UK, Europe, and Asia or for continuing education in the U.S.

Many dental schools and other influencers propose doing a CV for one reason or another. Their logic is usually sound, but with the widespread use of AI software, having both a résumé *and* a CV will be to your advantage. Let me explain. While the idea of crafting both a résumé and then a CV sounds time-consuming, the good news is that we'll spend the bulk of our time on drafting a résumé, and then use AI software to help with the conversion to a CV, saving you time and a likely headache. And that's what we're all about here at The Educated Associate.

As featured in an episode of *Last Week Tonight with John Oliver* (Season 8, Episode 15), AI software is being used for an astounding number of applications. Yes, *applications* has a double meaning here since AI software is literally auditing most job applications/résumés before humans ever see them.

Toward the end of my fourth year in dental school, I remember attending multiple lectures about drafting a CV. It was all about making it highly personalized so that it would "stick out to the reviewer." My 84 classmates and I all ended up with 84 different-looking CVs. I have no idea whose CV would perform best with modern AI software, but what I do know is that AI software performs best with simple, well-structured, chronological résumés that are easily read by a computer. This means to consider using the template included at the end of Chapter 13 which has been designed and successfully tested to get your résumé sent from the AI goalkeeper to the human associated with the job you've applied for.

Essentially, you need to compose a résumé that establishes that you're a dentist and that you want to start work within a given date range in a specific geographic area. It should also highlight any particular dental treatments that interest you or that you are already proficient in. That is it. You want the software to confirm that you match the avatar the corporation is looking to hire. You're not trying to "stand out from the stack" at this point; rather, you want your résumé to get to a human, by matching their goal avatar associate.

In my experience, the human gatekeeper at the associateship of your dreams will likely send you a pre-written email asking for you to submit your "résumé/CV and relevant documents" directly to him or her for review. This is the point at which having both a résumé and CV becomes very important. What most students do—and what I did early in my career—is submit the résumé again but this time to the person in the email. This person then ends up with the same form they've already obtained through Glassdoor or Indeed. Luckily, the dental market I was in was hungry for dentists, and my lazy approach didn't backfire. Later in my career, however, when transitioning to the highly competitive Phoenix dental market, I had to hone my technique.

Nowadays, upon secondary request, I submit a CV, not my résumé, and a cover letter directly to the employer. The CV can stay essentially the same between various offices, but the cover letter should *always* be tailored to the specific office and job to which you're applying. This is how you "jump off the stack" and look different from everyone else when it really matters—when human eyes are involved.

Now we'll discuss converting your résumé into a CV. When it comes to formatting your CV, be sure to use a professionally designed template, such as one from a reputable résumé builder. Nowadays, Microsoft Word has some highly effective templates that come free with the software. This will ensure that the layout of your CV looks polished and professional. It will also save you countless hours of formatting since this has all been standardized for you by the template. Bear in mind that the symmetry of the template is important to the overall aesthetic of the CV, which means you have to fight the urge to go moving things around. We're now looking to begin standing out to the reviewer, so look for something that has some style but is easy to read.

Creating a convincing CV requires more than just listing your qualifications, experience, and skills as with the simple résumé from the template included. Your CV should showcase your professional achievements in a way that follows your career path, demonstrates that you're the ideal candidate for the position, and makes it easy for recruiters to find the information they're looking for. When putting together your CV it should also include any awards or certificates you've received, which will give recruiters an indication of your abilities. Make sure you also include any professional memberships or affiliations that you have; these demonstrate to recruiters your commitment to staying up to date with current trends and developments in the field. Similarly, include any specialized experience or skills that you have. This could be any relevant coursework as well as certifications or qualifications in dentistry or healthcare-related fields.

Follow the simple steps below to convert your basic résumé into a document that underscores all the success you've had and is at the same time aesthetically pleasing to the reviewer.

1. Add a personal statement or objective at the beginning of the document that provides an overview of the entire CV. Tell them briefly who you are and what you're good at. The remainder of the CV will highlight technical items or skill sets, so use this section to provide that 30,000-foot overview of the entire document to come. Coming out of dental school, I really had no idea what specific procedures I was actually proficient in. I knew, however, that I was really good at dealing with anxious patients, so I used this brief paragraph to talk about this talent, which otherwise wouldn't have been conveyed until an in-person interview. I recommend using this section to highlight a subjective trait or two (LM). Are you exceptionally compassionate? Do you have excellent communication skills? Are you the best problem solver or the most patient person in any room? Use this section to underline some of those traits since this will get reviewers excited about you as they dig into the rest of your CV. If you are a poor writer or lack time, leverage ChatGPT to help you write this section. Obviously the more unique and honest you can make it, the better.

2. Expand the education section. Instead of simply listing your dental school and the date of graduation, include subsections/details that discuss relevant coursework,

especially if you're a graduate who didn't attend residency. Since you likely lack a clinical portfolio of cases, you should use this section to highlight things you did in dental school that make you look like an excellent student. For example, I listed my overall GPA as 3.69/4.0. This number looked better to me than my class rank, which was 33/84. Look at your GPA, class rank, special honors, and achievements and emphasize anything that makes dental school look like more than another degree on your CV. Again, you can consider using ChatGPT to help with the prose.

3. Add any professional certifications or licenses you may have earned. Be sure to include things relevant to dentistry, such as your Basic Life Support (BLS), board-certified DDS/ DMD, nitrous oxide certifications, Invisalign certifications, iTero-scan certifications, etc. This is a section where you can really stand out. If you did an extra training seminar and got a certification, list it.

4. You should spend a significant portion of time developing the section that discusses prior work/career experience. If you were a dental assistant, provide a detailed description of your duties and responsibilities. This section will grow rapidly once you obtain your first associateship. If you were like me and had absolutely no real-life experience as a paid employee in dentistry, then this is an opportunity to flex your creative genius. I was once a medical assistant (never a dental assistant) at a cardiology office. I used this section to discuss how I spent countless hours working with patients in some of the direst situations they'd ever faced. I described how I was able to hone my ability to help anxious patients heading into open-heart surgeries and expanded that concept into dentistry, where, while still in dental school, I was often given the most anxious patients. As a student, I gained a reputation for being good with anxious patients and was able to tie the education section

on my CV to my prior job experience. This is also a way to tie your personal statement into the CV, making it a high-yield section that the reviewer will actually read. Spending time developing a consistent message in the CV helps ensure that you project your chosen self-image ahead of your interviews.

5. Add a section for your professional memberships and affiliations as well as for services you take part in. You can expand this section by including your positions within these organizations. For example, I was vice president and treasurer for AO Dental Fraternity while in school. I am now a board member for a nonprofit in New Mexico called Dental Care in Your Home. I added these as well as a brief explanation of my duties to the CV.

6. Add a section for volunteer work if that applies.

7. If you are a recent graduate, a section with relevant skills may be helpful. Include technical skills, such as using CAD/CAM software, as well as soft skills, such as communication, to show the employer what you're proficient in. If you can provide brief explanations, that can be useful as well.

8. Add a list of references to whom the employer can speak about your skills, experience, and character. Your references may consist only of dental school instructors, but that's OK. My list of four references included three attending doctors at the University of Colorado and the cardiologist I worked for in Denver. I think it's best if the references are involved in healthcare.

Now that you have successfully created both a résumé and a CV, you are ready to start applying, which we will cover next. Remember, the purpose of the résumé is to get through the sea of AI software used by job websites like Indeed and Glassdoor. Once you know you fit the avatar the hiring office wants, deploy the CV, which the humans in the actual office will review and love. If you are ready to learn about applying, read on to Chapter 5!

Chapter Summary Points:

1. Consider the "Résumé Funnel" approach to associateship application

2. First, use an included template to make an AI-readable résumé—basic is best

3. Submit this basic résumé to your online job applications

4. Now leverage ChatGPT to turn the résumé into a CV

5. Submit the CV to the actual office staff for human review

Chapter 5

Applying for Your Dream Associateship

We started this journey by deciding what the perfect office/owner would look like for you by describing an avatar. We then delved into determining whether a DSO, private practice, or nonprofit practice is best for you. Next we targeted your search and found opportunities that seem to match the type of practice best suited for you. Then we created a simple but AI-readable résumé, which we converted to a more specific CV that we'll use in the coming steps to help you stick out to possible employers. Reading that sounds like we have completed a lot, and we sure have, but there are more steps to get you the job of your dreams. We've now graduated from basic training and are ready for the battle of applying for and negotiating your dream contract. This is where the big money can be made, so let's jump right in.

If you don't have any in-person leads, then start back on Indeed and Glassdoor. You'll have to create an account and set the geographic parameters. I suggest checking these web pages at least twice a week. The best times to check are Sunday evening and Wednesday morning because this is when most new jobs first get posted. It really helps to be the first to apply to a newly listed opening. Even if you aren't the perfect candidate, they're looking to hire but you're first means you're more likely to get a thorough review. Like Wayne Gretzky said, "You miss 100% of the shots you don't take." Just apply if you think there is a chance you might love the job regardless of the specific requirements listed in the ad. There really is no risk to you other than hearing the word, "no". Always ask (LM)!

Once you find several appealing opportunities, submit your basic résumé through the web page. The websites, for some reason, seem to transport your résumé, which is in a Word document, into some template specific to the website itself. It's important to check over the résumé template created by the website for errors because the web page software may move some information around. This is why a simple and chronological résumé is best— it's easy for the website to work with. Once you approve the template, the website will start running your résumé through their AI software to match you with other possible employers beyond the position you just applied for. You should hear back within three days of submitting the résumé if the company you applied for is interested in you. Additionally, in this time, several other offices may reach out based on the AI matching functions intrinsic to the website. If you are applying to a private practice and you hear from that office, it is typically an office manager reaching out to you via email and asking for your résumé. I suppose they probably don't want the résumé in the template form from the website, so they reach out to you for the Word document, which is more reader friendly. This is the perfect opportunity to impress the office manager by submitting your CV, which is an eye-pleaser, as well as a cover letter tailored to their specific practice as opposed to just sending them your résumé in Word document form. At last, the "résumé funnel" has come full circle, or top to bottom, or however funnels work these days!

The key part of the paragraph above is the office-specific cover letter. For the entire application and interview process you can keep your résumé and CV virtually the same between offices because it is describing you, which isn't changing. On the other hand, the office you are applying to is changing with each office and every office is different. The nuance differences among dental offices are what make each office unique and are the reason for the cover letter. The cover letter is your chance to showcase all the things that stuck out to you about the office or owner(s) themselves. You can do research on the practice website as well as social media. Anything you can detect about the owners' hobbies or interests could also be brought up in the cover letter. Additionally, if they have lots of technology and you love scanning, designing, and milling your own crowns, then bring up the advanced technology and your affinity for it in the cover letter. This lets the office know that you did your due diligence to understand them. Believe it or not, people love being noticed for their individuality. Furthermore, practice owners love cover letters that talk about how their office is great and how you could make it stronger. The cover letter is your chance to showcase that.

When writing a cover letter for a specific dental office, it is important to address the hiring manager or the dentist you are reaching out to. Showcase your relevant experience and skills, express your enthusiasm for the position and the office, and explain how you can contribute to their team. It is crucial to tailor your cover letter to demonstrate how your qualifications align with the specific needs of the dental office. If you can demonstrate this, you will get an interview.

A well-written cover letter should be no longer than one page while using a professional and easy-to-read font. Be sure to include your contact information and encourage the hiring manager to review your CV for more detailed information about your qualifications. You should submit your CV and office-specific cover letter to the hiring office when they inquire initially.

At this point the CV is now in the office manager's hands, and you know they're interested in you since they asked for more information directly from you, so you can rest assured they'll review the CV and cover letter in detail. All that time you spent developing your unique characteristics in the personal statement at the top of the CV will make you jump off the stack. Additionally, the cover letter gives you a chance to tell them in detail why you're a great fit for *their* practice. This is why each cover letter is different—it needs to be specific to that office, not offices generally. The specificity of the cover letter will make the office manager and owner happy because you have basically talked them up in the letter itself. Be as specific as possible. This shows that you spent time reviewing their individual practice and tells the office manager how enthusiastic you are about joining their staff. For example, if they talk about being high-tech on their website, maybe bring up your excitement to use their intraoral scanner for in-house milling of indirect restorations. Even if you aren't *exactly* the candidate they're searching for, having all these personal details will likely keep you in contention for the position. We're using the résumé funnel to ensure that you get a chance to interview. My belief is that if we can get you in front of the owner at your dream office, then your wonderful and matching personalities should take over from there. The résumé funnel is a means to that end.

If you don't hear back within three days of sending in your CV and cover letter, you should follow up with an email or text message. Again, this shows how serious you are about the opportunity. It will also put your name in front of the office manager again, which can be helpful if another candidate falls through later in the process. The OM may remember you and schedule you for an interview—because you reached out just one more time. Again, you never get punished for taking a shot; you only guarantee yourself failure if you don't try.

Alternatively, there's the recruitment strategy employed by most DSOs, especially the larger ones. The first person you're likely to interact with outside Indeed or Glassdoor in the DSO is a recruiter rather than the OM from the example described above. The recruiter is essentially a salesperson for the DSO. They're there to give you some basic details and see whether you're interested in the job opportunity. Like any salesman, they excel at making the DSO sound great.

More often than not, the goal of the recruiter is to see whether you're interested in talking with some higher-level recruiter or someone more specific to the area in which they hope to employ you. This next person may be a regional director or an individual at the office trying to hire an associate. The initial talks with the recruiter almost always go the same route: *Tell me about yourself. What procedures do you like? Which ones don't you like?* They will then dive into the corporate mission and the ways in which they help their doctors. Next, they'll lay out basic benefits from the employee handbook and tell you about contract items that may be nonnegotiable. In the middle of a meeting with a recruiter, I was told associates would be responsible for a 50% lab fee, which was nonnegotiable. This was a deal-breaker for me, and I told the recruiter. She still spent another 10 minutes trying to convince me to just meet with the regional director. I declined.

In hindsight my viewpoint has since changed about turning down initial job opportunities before being offered a physical contract. Early in your career, having options puts you in a better position than merely feeling good about turning down an offer, like I had done, even if it isn't ideal (LM). Side note: In the contract negotiations section, we'll discuss how to work around these "nonnegotiable" items. Everything is negotiable! You just need the right approach.

If you choose to continue the process with the DSO, you'll likely meet with someone who knows many more specifics about the actual job you've set your sights on. The initial recruiter likely knows nothing about the clinical setting of the specific office or has never even met with a person working there. This second-level person is likely to have been on the ground at this office. He or she will know many more specifics, such as whether they have CBCT, what kind of implants they use, and other clinical details. This is also someone whose sole purpose is to get an applicant to the next level of the interview process within the DSO. They, like the first recruiter, probably get paid for leads.

You are the lead, so be sure to dig deep. Get some details about the office beyond what can be found online. I'd encourage you to ask difficult questions, the kind you may even be reluctant to ask the office staff if you plan to continue on to an in-person interview. For example, if the DSO pays based on collections, I often ask whether they're willing to provide verification of collections, etc. I'd also dig into what percentage of the office's patient population is insurance-based, and then beyond that what specific insurance companies the office accepts. Really investigate Medicaid, Medicare, Large Dental Insurer, and HMO plans as well as the percentage of the office's patients that are composed by these carriers. These answers may have a larger effect on your future earning potential than anything else at the physical office. I've found it much less uncomfortable asking this recruiter these difficult financial questions as opposed to waiting and asking someone in-person at the physical office, which can feel very awkward. Just know that at some point, you will need to ask these questions; getting them out of the way early has been like lifting a weight off my chest. Not only do you feel better about asking those difficult questions, but you know the answer to them now as well. So, you can feel much more confident that you won't be wasting your time if you continue to pursue the office for an in-person interview since you understand the financial situation of the office. If you liked what you heard from this regional recruiter and conversely, they still like you, then you will likely be offered a job or asked for an in-person interview.

Now, we have discussed the two most common pathways for an interviewee to make their way from submitting an application to a proposed in-person interview, the private practice/office manager pathway and the DSO/ recruiter pathway. Whether you've been chosen to interview at a DSO, private practice, or both, the next steps are very similar. Come with me as we learn to interview at your dream office together.

Chapter Summary Points:

1. Create an account on Indeed or Glassdoor

2. Apply for jobs, even if you don't think you are the ideal candidate

3. Thoroughly check the résumé you submit to the website for errors when the site processes it into a template

4. Send your CV and a well-written cover letter, specific to THAT office, to the OM (private practice) or recruiter (DSO), completing the résumé funnel

5. Reach out to any office you don't hear back from after three days to show your interest

Chapter 6

Interviewing at Your Dream Job

Once you have an interview request, you should be excited; you officially have a foot in a dental office's door. Next, we'll discuss getting ready for the interview both physically and mentally. At the end of this chapter, you'll find a list of common interview questions for associates. I don't necessarily recommend writing down preloaded responses to these questions, although that is helpful if you are an anxious interviewee. Practice really does make perfect. Instead, I at a minimum make sure I've thought over some answers to the questions so they don't catch me by surprise. I do this before each interview and have for years now. Eventually the review will take no more than a few minutes, but initially I would spend a half hour or so thinking through some responses. If you know there's a specific question or style of question that you struggle with, then practicing a response to that specific question would be well worth your time. I utilize my wife, who is a great interviewer and interviewee to ask me some of the difficult questions the night before the interview for practice. We practice for 15–20 minutes; I build my confidence and get to spend some time with the wife. It's a win-win-win and great for pre-interview nerves.

I also find it vital to have a handful of questions that you'd like to ask them during the interview. I tend to write down three to five very specific questions to ask the OM or practice owner. These questions need to be specific to the company with which you're interviewing. An example from one of my past interviews is "I saw that you did a residency at the University of Colorado and that Dr. XYZ was the preceptor of the program at that time, as he is now.

Did he teach you guys about giving the Gow-Gates block as well?" Everyone likes talking about themselves, so by asking personal questions you're getting the owner to feel good about themselves while also uncovering some information. In other words, by asking a very specific set of questions, you'll learn more about your potential boss while also "buttering them up" by showing how much interest you have in them and their practice.

Now that we have jogged our brains in preparation for the interview, the next thing we will discusses is getting dressed. In dental school we were taught to don and doff our surgical attire like a gown and gloves, but little discussion was made into what to wear to future interviews. I hope to provide some clarity on what I wore and what representatives at several higher-end professional clothing stores recommended to me or my wife before we interviewed.

<u>Outfit Selection</u>

The next step is to select your outfit for the interview. I've talked with the men's-suits sales associates at Men's Wearhouse and Jos. A. Bank. According to them, men should interview in a dark suit. Most recommend a black, dark-blue, or charcoal-gray suit with a simple, light-colored button-down underneath. The tie should be conservative (no flashy patterns). Leather shoes are preferred, but dark sneakers that are clean could also be considered. As a general rule, keep accessories such as watches, earrings, or other jewelry to a minimum.

Remember, the goal is to look professional and polished, so clothes that fit well and are pressed are your priority. Also, be sure they are comfortable since an interview may go on for several hours. We've all seen or been the guy with the all-day wedgie from professional clothes that only get pulled out of the closet twice a year. I suggest trying on your outfit and making sure that it's comfortable. The last thing you need is to be dealing with that annoying wedgie while trying to land your dream associateship.

For women, the concept is similar, but like most social things it tends to be more complicated for women than men. I'll start by saying, I am no expert in clothes, and I am certainly no expert in women's clothing. My wife, a pediatrician, went to Banana Republic to select an outfit for her interviews. I spoke with a stylist there who suggested choosing something polished, professional, and well-fitted. Wear a solid-colored suit or conservative dress with a jacket. Muted colors are preferred. Avoid flashy jewelry and bold patterns. Go with comfortable shoes that have at most a moderately high heel. Keeping your hairstyle simple, your makeup natural, and avoiding strong fragrances can all make for a strong first impression. All in all, put together an outfit that makes you feel good about yourself. Again, I am not an expert on women's clothing, and the best advice I can give you is to be comfortable or seek professional help at a store of your choosing.

Finishing Touches Before Interviewing

Some final things to do before the actual interview: Print several copies of your CV and any professional certificates listed on your CV along with a copy of your diploma or state dental license (if applicable). This will show the office how organized you are. Moreover, it demonstrates a willingness to take initiative. I've found simply bringing in copies of these documents to be a real icebreaker. The owners are often impressed by my foresight and my printed-out certificates, which make it look like I accomplished a lot while in dental school (even if every student in my class boasts the same certificates). The small stack of certificates acts as a reminder to the owner that you're an overachiever. The physical fact of paper copies is a much stronger psychological lever than a list on your CV; the owner will take notice (LM).

Now that you've chosen your outfit, prepared several questions for the owner, thought out some possible replies to interview questions, and printed your documents, all that's left to do is show up for the interview. Show up at least 10 minutes early, present yourself professionally (starting when you leave the parking lot), and maintain excellent hygiene. Aside from this, I encourage you to be yourself. You've already cleared the highest hurdles: finding the dream office, tailoring a cover letter to the dream office, and sending an email or making a phone call to land an in-person interview. They clearly like the person you presented online and via documentation, so take a deep breath, sit down with me, and in the next paragraph we'll discuss the interview.

<u>The Interview</u>

I've interviewed for 15–20 different dental associateships since graduating from dental school. Overall, it's been a fairly even mix of DSOs and private practices. In my experience the following scenario is the most consistent part of the interview process: You show up to the office. More likely than not, the office manager or recruiting coordinator will be the one who greets you. They will either show you the office (think tour) or take you to their specific office to conduct an interview. You'll probably get blasted with typical interview questions and requests, such as *tell me about yourself.* Think of this as the more formal interview.

After the tour and interview with the OM, they'll ask you—if they approve of you—to meet the owner. In every single one of my interviews, I've been asked to meet with the owner. This is where the rubber meets the road. At this point the owner is simply there to make sure they can work with you. The OM has already audited you on paper and vetted you in person. The owner trusts the OM to do this background work. They are no longer concerned with your credentials or with minor details on your CV the way the office manager was. The owner is there to make sure they can see themselves working next to you four to five days a week, especially in a private practice setting.

Believe it or not, an owner I met with once pulled out a beer during this phase of the interview. It was a Friday afternoon, and

I could tell all he wanted to do was make sure he could get along with me. To him, that meant making sure he could drink a beer around me and have a conversation. We talked college baseball, and he offered me the job on the way out.

Try not to get caught up in semantics. This, by the way, was an excellent opportunity for me to see how the owner would behave as well (LM). After a long week of work, having a beer and talking baseball sounded perfect, so I knew we'd be a good fit. On the other hand, if you don't drink alcohol or watch sports, a similar situation might make you uncomfortable—maybe this isn't the ideal associateship for you. My best advice is to be yourself and make certain you can see yourself working next to the owner day in and day out.

At this point there are three directions in which the deal could head. The owner could offer you the job right there on the spot; they could say they'll get back to you in XX days and send a contract via email; or they could offer a contract to someone else.

Even if you aren't offered a contract on the spot or within the first week after the interview, you're not ruled out of the job until you receive an email stating that the office has gone "in another direction." They may be interviewing more candidates. Stay positive! I encourage students always to write a follow-up email or, better yet, a formal, handwritten letter thanking the OM and owner for having you to their office. Just as your cover letter was specific to that office, the more specific you can make this handwritten sentiment, the more power it will have.

The power of the handwritten thank-you card is multifaceted. Firstly, it reiterates your interest in the position and shows you'll go the extra mile to get what you want. Second, it shows your willingness to do things others won't, such as use a form of communication that requires a good deal more effort than the email most of your peers will send. Another powerful reason to send a handwritten thank-you card is to restate things from the interview. In Season 4 and Episode 4, from the TV series *Parks and Recreation*, the main character writes a note to her prospective employer, thanking him for interviewing her and apologizing for arguing with him. While the series is poking fun at the situation, she's able to restructure the reason she argued with him and ends up getting the job. While I wouldn't suggest a blow-up with your interviewer, sending a handwritten follow-up can be exceptionally useful if part of the conversation didn't go the way you would've liked. In general, staying positive and following up will be your next steps if you still want to work for the employer with whom you interviewed.

<u>Receiving an Offer</u>

Now we'll discuss receiving an offer, whether at the interview or via email. Don't forget: No contract is official until there's a signed document. Handshake promises mean nothing—always remember that. Get it in writing and have both of you sign it; then it carries legal ramifications for both of you (LM). That said, in my experience if the owner is interested in offering you the position, at least a portion of your interview will focus on basic compensation structure, how patients get divided up between providers, and maybe even employee benefits (if any). So, if they start talking pay, get excited because they must like you so far. At this point being agreeable is the strategy I recommend unless they start low-balling you. Try to get the gist of what the offer entails and maintain your composure (hearing about your possible future earnings can feel a bit surreal). I even took notes during some of my initial interviews because I wanted to compare what they told me in the interview with the terms of the contract that would later be emailed to me. This is another way to ensure that the owner is being honest and consistent. It would for sure be a red flag if they don't align ⚑ .

Now all that's left to do now is sit back and wait for the contract to land in your inbox. Soon the fun aspect of contract negotiations will get going, but first, in the next chapter, we will look at basic associate agreements so we can understand the nuts and bolts of what should and shouldn't be there. We will start by discussing associate pay types first. Once we understand an agreement, we can negotiate it effectively!

<u>Grilling the Dentist:</u> Common Interview Questions and How to Answer Them

1. Why don't you tell me about yourself?
2. Why did you decide to become a dentist?
3. How skilled are you in dealing with dental emergencies?
4. What specific procedures have you performed as a dentist?
5. How comfortable are you with operating sophisticated dental equipment?
6. How would you handle an uncooperative patient during a procedure?
7. Have you ever had any special training to ensure your success in dentistry?
8. Are there any techniques or practices that you feel strongly about when treating patients?
9. Describe the biggest challenge you've faced treating patients; how did it turn out?
10. What do you think sets you apart from other dentists?
11. What experience do you have in dealing with children's dental issues?
12. How familiar are you with the most up-to-date protocols and procedures for providing dental care?
13. Do you feel comfortable working with a diverse array of patients, ages, and backgrounds?
14. Are there any particular methods that you use to ensure patient satisfaction throughout the treatment process?
15. Do you have experience educating patients about oral hygiene practices or other dental-related topics?
16. Describe an example of a successful treatment plan that resulted in a positive outcome for the patient.

17. In your opinion, what's the most important factor in providing quality dental care?
18. Tell me about a difficult clinical case; how did you handle it?
19. What strategies do you use to stay abreast of advances in dentistry?
20. Are there any changes that you would make to improve the patient experience?
21. How do you handle difficult patients?
22. How would you explain complex dental conditions or treatments to patients with limited understanding of medical terminology?
23. Describe your approach to ensuring accurate record-keeping for patient files.
24. Have you ever worked as part of a dental team, and what did that involve?
25. Do you have any questions for me?

<u>General Guidelines for Answering Interview Questions:</u>

1. Tell me about a time when …

    a. STAR Method – Situation, Task, Action, and Result

        i. Situation – Describe a specific situation

        ii. Task – What was the goal you were trying to achieve? Describe it

        iii. Action – The specific actions you took to address the situation; focus on YOU!

        iv. Result – How your actions resulted in the final outcome

    b. Example: "Tell me about a time when you had to manage a difficult patient."

        i. Situation: I was working at an urban clinic on an away rotation in dental school when a young adult male came in for his routine appointment. I discovered an infected tooth that needed treatment.

    ii.   Task: He didn't believe he had an infection, and I had the difficult task of persuading him to allow me to perform a procedure.

    iii.   Action: I used a combination of empathy and firmness by first sympathizing with his reluctance to accept treatment and then explaining why it was necessary for his health. I spoke calmly and reassuringly, illustrating my point with personal stories so he could relate.

    iv.   Result: Ultimately, I convinced him to agree to the treatment, and he had a successful RCT and crown. After the procedure, I followed up with the patient to make sure he was doing better. During a follow-up visit, he opened up and thanked me for helping him out of a tough spot.

Impressive Questions to Ask the Employer:

1. Can you describe a typical day for an associate here?

2. What do you expect me to complete in my first 90 days?

3. How long have you been with this company? What has kept you here?

4. What do you like to do in your spare time?

5. What are some attributes of the best associates you've had in the past?

6. How would you describe the work environment/corporate culture?

7. What are some of the short- and long-term goals the company has for me?

8. What are some short- and long-term goals the company has for itself?

Chapter Summary Points:

1. Prepare for your interview by answering practice questions

2. Prepare for your interview by composing some questions to ask the owner or OM

3. Select a comfortable outfit that makes you proud to be a professional

4. Print out physical copies of your diplomas, certificates, CV, and cover letter to bring to the office

5. Show up 10 minutes early

6. Remember no contract is official until there is a document signed by you and your employer

Chapter 7

Associate Pay Types

Before diving into how to talk with the owner and how to negotiate effectively, we have to lay some basic contractual groundwork. If you go into negotiations without an understanding of how the owner is actually going to pay you, then you're going to get taken for a contractual ride. So let's have a brief discussion about the most common associate-dentist pay structures. In general, there are three main ways associates get paid: based on collections, based on simple production, or based on adjusted production.

As we dive further into these contract terms, you'll begin to see how an owner might say, in the face-to-face interview, that they're paying you "on production," when according to the terms of the actual contract, your pay *feels* entirely collections-based via the adjusted-production model. That said, I don't want you to think collections-based contracts are inherently bad. In truth, any contract can be rewarding. I've seen collections contracts that, when compared to the adjusted-production contracts typical of the same geographical area, were financially more favorable for an associate. However, it's equally possible a given contract will take you for a ride—and not a fun one (as alluded to above). Collections contracts are the easiest to discuss, so we'll start there.

Put simply, collections is the total amount of money collected by a dental office, paid either by patients or an insurance company, as compensation for dental services (rendered by a specific dentist/hygienist). Associate-dentist contracts state the specific percentage of collections that the associate will receive as payment for work they specifically provided. Let's review a few examples to provide clarity.

Example Baseline:

Let's say you've signed an associateship contract with a pay structure that states that your compensation will be 30% of collections. A new-patient comprehensive exam (COE) – D0150 may bill for $100 at that specific office. This is known as the UCR fee (fee the office charges if there's no insurance contract). In this example, the contracted fee with Large Dental Insurer for a COE is $50.

Example One:

If you complete a COE on a patient without insurance (fee for service), the office should collect $100 (the UCR fee) prior to the patient being seen for the exam. The office therefore collected at 100% of the UCR fee, and you'll be paid, pre-tax, $30. There are no write-offs. As the associate dentist, you can be paid your portion of the dental service in the current pay period.

Example Two:

You completed the COE on a Large Dental Insurer patient. The patient owes nothing at the time of service, and the office submits a claim to Large Dental Insurer for the service you provided. You and the office are likely paid nothing from the insurance company in the current pay period for the above treatment (it takes time to process claims). Several weeks later the office obtains a reimbursement for the COE but at the contracted rate of $50. The office you work for now claims a tax write-off on the $50 that the insurance already "wrote-off" themselves (UCR fee – reimbursed fee = write-off). You'll be paid just $15: 30% of the $50 that was collected ($50 x 0.3 = $15). The office will still maintain that they collected at "100% collections rate," claim a tax write-off (as did the insurance company), and the associate is stuck earning substantially less, getting paid in a later pay period, and receiving no personal tax incentives (W-2 contract specifically). The main difference between adjusted production and collections here is *when* the associate gets paid. Adjusted allows the associate to be paid earlier, in the pay period when the service was rendered and often *before* the office obtains reimbursement. Again, on collections contracts the associate is paid *after* the office has received the money. Another work-around for when the associate gets paid is the "draw." More on the draw shortly.

Many owners justify using collections-based associate pay by saying "it aligns the associate's interests with those of the practice since both parties benefit from increased collections." I've also heard owners say things like, "It teaches young doctors the most important aspect of owning a business, which is to collect the money." To me, this is illogical. You're the associate, not the owner. Why would any associate worry about something they have absolutely no control over? Unless the owner plans to give you authority to change office collections principles, an owner giving you the above reasoning for collections-based pay strikes me as a big red flag ▶ .

Moreover, how does the dentistry equivalent of commission-production-based pay not align an associate's goals with those of the practice? Quite literally, the goal of generating more revenue as an associate directly results in increased net profit for the owner as long as they are holding up their end of the deal by collecting. On top of that, I'm not a fan of owners acting like my father by using a contract to teach me something pejoratively. The owner is there to manage the business and collect money, while you're there to complete dentistry. The contract should also align these goals.

Now, back to my original point: Collections contracts are not inherently bad. If the office can demonstrate a reasonably high collections rate (96% or higher), then collections and adjusted-production contracts can be very comparable. I'd encourage you to ask for some kind of documentation verifying collections as soon as you know they want to pay associates based on collections or adjusted production. If you deal with an OM or recruiter early on, ask them for verification, which won't feel as awkward as asking the business owner during the interview as mentioned a few chapters ago.

Although there's no set collections rate I find acceptable across all markets, 96% or above would make the contract worth further consideration in my mind. Furthermore, any office using basic billing software can pull up these financial numbers with little or no effort, so you really aren't asking for much when you ask for verification. Daily, I pull up my production/collection numbers where I work to keep track of how I'm doing. More importantly, if there's more than one doctor working in the same office, I keep tabs on whom procedures/claims are being billed under. Sometimes mistakes happen with the billing department, and the exam you did on Mrs. Smith gets billed under the owning doctor rather than yourself. It's best to catch these issues the day they occur rather than down the road (LM).

In terms of verifying collections, I ask for the three top revenue-grossing dental treatments (e.g., dental porcelain crown–D2740, resin-based composite/two surface-posterior–D2393, etc.), what the specific UCR is for these treatments, and what is typically collected from fee-for-service-paying patients as well as from their three top insurance providers. Always include Large Dental Insurers as well as HMO plans since these are known for reimbursement rates that may amount to less than 50% of the invoiced costs. This is where the whole idea of simple production vs. adjusted-production vs. collections comes into play, which we'll look into further ahead.

On the surface level, a contract based on collections should always pay the associate at a higher percentage than any production-based contract when compared across similar patient demographics. As a rule, if associates are typically paid ~30% of adjusted production within a specific geographic area, then collections pay would likely need to be 5% higher, or ~35%, in order for the associate to earn a similar amount. So if you receive a contract offer for 30% of adjusted production and another office offers 30% of collections, the offer for collections is a worse financial contract: You'll earn less if patient demographics are similar. The key phrase here is "patient demographics." If the offices have different patient profiles, then the pay structures are less comparable. This is an area where you should do your own due diligence during the interview process.

In reality there are very few contracts that are truly based on production alone—i.e., with no adjustments. I think many students for some reason enter the dental field expecting the above type of associate payment to be the norm, but it's not. For an office to pay you this way, it would most likely have to be a cash-only or fee-for-service type office, no insurance reimbursement accepted. The patients who receive treatments are then responsible for 100% of payment at the time of service. This is like a spa: You walk in, pay for a service, receive the service, and leave. An operation like this makes paying the associate based on production alone possible since no adjustments need to be made for either party because production should equal collections daily.

Obviously, this is a perfect-world scenario for associate pay. While there are offices that operate this way, they are the exception, especially in urban areas. If you want to work in a rural area, this may be a viable option out of dental school/residency. In my experience, fee-for-service clinics in urban areas are privately owned, are offices mostly with single/dual doctors' structures, and if they're seeking an associate, they often want a minimum of five years of experience. If this type of pay is really all you want out of your first associateship, plan on searching for a much longer period of time because, while you may find one, this is really a needle in a haystack for new grads.

On the other hand, in most dental offices some level of insurance is accepted, and you will therefore likely be paid based on adjusted production. Some offices take PPO plans alone, while others take plans such as HMOs as well. Look for Chapter 12 discussing various insurances, but for now all that insurance really means for you is *adjustments*. From a 10,000-foot view, different insurance companies have negotiated contracts with different dental offices and vice versa. Essentially, the dental office agrees to provide a specific dental service for a specific fee with a specific dental-insurance company. This could mean that the office typically charges a $1,000 UCR fee for a dental crown (your cash-pay fee), while the negotiated deal with Large Dental Insurer is to reimburse crowns at $476 per unit. At the same time, the negotiated fee with Presbyterian PPO is $976. The fees can vary greatly, as shown above.

On paper this could mean that when you deliver a crown approved by Large Dental Insurer to a patient, the production figure on the day sheet will read $1,000 for the crown (UCR fee only). The patient will have paid $0. Therefore, $0 of the $1,000 UCR fee has been collected upon the completion of the treatment. The office staff and likely a billing company will team up and submit a claim to Large Dental Insurer that you completed a service for which you have a negotiated contract. The insurance company will look for any reason not to reimburse the office. If you follow all the insurance companies' rules, the office will get a check for the negotiated fee, in this case $476, about a month or so later.

Meanwhile, the office where you work if you have an adjusted production pay structure likely paid you ~30% of the UCR fee ($1,000) while waiting for reimbursement from large dental insurer. This is where the "adjustments" come into play. When the office gets paid the $476, they adjust the difference, i.e., $524, in your next paycheck. This doesn't mean you owe the office $524; it means the office will treat $524 as a tax write-off. For now, you can think of write-offs as a benefit to business owners or workers who are paid as independent contractors (IRS form 1099) rather than W-2 employees.

To continue the example above, if you produce $10,000 during the next pay cycle, the office subtracts $524 from your gross production of $10,000, making your adjusted production for that pay period $9,476. All in all, the adjustment reduced your pay during a subsequent pay period. In my experience, the more insurance companies the office is contracted with, the more difficult it becomes to track these adjustments. Moreover, the amount written off/adjusted can become a shocking percentage of a future pay period depending on how many claims are paid during that subsequent period—all of which is likely out of your control.

If you break down the above example further, the office *really* collected below 50% of their UCR fee but collected 100% of their negotiated fee with Large Dental Insurer. The office can then tell you they have nearly 100% collections overall. To me, this is far from true unless they're somehow collecting the $524 difference from the patients themselves. While the office can have patients sign a form stating they're responsible for what insurance doesn't cover up to the UCR fee, this can quickly get tricky from a legal standpoint and is way outside the purpose of this writing. To me, the office really has a below 50% collections rate on Large Dental Insurer patients, but instead of paying you on something they didn't receive themselves, they simply pass the financial burden down to the associate (LM). It's a win-win for the office and lose-lose for associates and is a major driver of associates wanting to leave associateships and own their own practices these days.

At this time, it should be clear that if you are to be paid based on adjusted production, there are several very important things to pay attention to. First, what percentage of the patients in the office are insurance-based patients? You'll only be subject to adjustments when you treat insurance-based patients if the office has excellent collecting policies, so knowing the percentage of patients with dental insurance can give you an idea of your potential reimbursements. Second, and to expand on the first, what percentage of patients are with Large Dental Insurer or an HMO? Large Dental Insurer and HMOs are well known for exceedingly low reimbursements, so knowing this percentage can help you judge your potential earnings in the office. Think about the example above in which Large Dental Insurer has a negotiated fee less than 50% of the UCR fee. As a reminder, a high percentage of Large Dental Insurer patients isn't inherently a contract-breaker, but I'd expect higher than 30% of adjusted production if Large Dental Insurer patients comprise more than 50% of the office's baseline. There are always ways to make a contract beneficial—we just need to negotiate the numbers.

Next, how does the office divvy up patients if it's a multiple-doctor practice? I've heard horror stories about associates who saw all the Large Dental Insurer and HMO patients, while the owner saw 100% of PPO and cash-only patients. This could be a financial nightmare for a new doctor. Make sure you clarify how new patients and exams are split up. Also, make sure you perform the treatments recommended by yourself. I've also heard stories of offices that have an owner do all the diagnosing and the indirect restorations while an associate does the direct restorations (recommended by the owner). Again, this will almost certainly be a poor financial situation to find yourself in. Be sure to clarify how you'll get the patients you'll be treating. As previously suggested, I'd ask for verification of the production, write-offs, and overall adjusted production of the previous associate before signing the contract (LM).

In my first year out of school, I typically produced ~$10,000–$15,000 per week. I was paid biweekly on an adjusted production model. I remember one case that involved 12 indirect units on Large Dental Insurer patient(s). The UCR fee was around $12,000, and the office paid me 30% of the $12,000, which was great for that pay period. Later, Large Dental Insurerreimbursed the office at around $5,000. I then had over $6,000 of production adjusted away all at once. To make matters worse, I was out sick for two days and only produced about $6,000 that week. Basically, on paper, I worked for three days but didn't get paid for it due to the timing of the adjustments compounded by my illness. Therefore, if you are the sole earner for your family, having an unpredictable income like this can cause some sleepless nights. So plan ahead with a budget when you are to be overcompensated in one pay period and then adjusted away in the subsequent one (LM). Look out for my next project on this very topic!

Adjustments will additionally be of importance when you give notice that you plan to leave the associateship. The contract should lay out how you'll be paid on your way out, but essentially, the office tends to pay out less on treatments toward the end of your time there since they need to account for adjustments after your last day. Be sure to really dig into this section when you're bracing yourself to hand in your notice.

Just to set the record straight, an office that's based 100% on dental insurance, has an associate paid on adjusted production, and has an overall collections rate of about 96% is essentially paying you on collections without using that term in your contract. I wish I had a dollar for every time someone asked me whether they should decline a contract because the office wanted to pay them based on collections when they had another offer for adjusted production. As I mentioned earlier, a contract that bases associate pay on collections is not an automatic "no" in my book. Every contract has the potential to be good; you just have to examine it and the office thoroughly. Some, of course, will be bad, while others are downright despicable.

Typically, when I see the term *collections* being used in a contract, that tells me the office is heavily dependent on insurance reimbursements. The office owner understands that every insurance company they contract with will offer different reimbursement rates and have different rules regarding what needs to be clinically present/completed in order to be reimbursed. For example, in New Mexico if there's no radiographic evidence of bone loss of at least 2 mm on all bite-wing radiographs, Large Dental Insurer will decline all full-quadrant SRP prior authorizations and any submitted claims for completed SRP treatments. Clinically, there might be advanced probing depths and the presence of radiographic calculus, but if there isn't at least 2 mm of alveolus loss, then SRPs will be denied. It's just their rule. If your office contracts with them, you'll need to learn this rule to make sure the treatments that you recommend will be reimbursed. There are rules like this for every treatment. You need to learn them all. Insurance can really be the bane of dentistry.

By paying you on the collections, the owner is simply passing the burden of learning these rules down to you. If you don't learn the insurance rules and you complete an uncovered dental service on a patient unwilling to pay themselves, it won't hurt the owner financially; they simply won't pay you for non-reimbursed work. Essentially, you can count that SRP you completed on a patient without bone loss as practice because no one's getting paid for it.

Now for a discussion on another associate pay structure and as promised, the draw. Essentially, a draw is a payment made to a contractor prior to the completion of a project (or collection of payments). The amount of draw is usually based on the percentage of work completed/collected, and it's meant to provide the contractor with consistent and predictable cash flow to continue working. Once the project/treatment is finished or monies are collected, the total amount of the draw is deducted from the final payment and things get squared up.

In dentistry, this means the contractor is the associate dentist and he or she is often paid a draw on a biweekly/ monthly basis. This draw assumes a normal anticipated collection rate for the dentist. The dentist can then be paid a consistent amount during the entire calendar quarter of work (regardless of whether they are even at work or not). This then feels like a salary; however, the difference lies at the end of the calendar quarter, when the financials are squared up. If the associate produced/collected more than the draw already paid, they receive a bonus. On the other hand, if the associate has actually collected less than what has already been paid out as a draw, then a deficiency is created. There are several ways various agreements handle deficiencies, but that is beyond the scope of this discussion.

Just for reference, at the time of this writing, I had been paid for about a year's time on a draw. It worked great for me as it allowed for more predictable budgeting during the year. I formed a bonus on one occasion, was in a small deficiency once, and was within $1,000 of the drawn amount on two other occasions, so it was basically even when we squared up quarterly. Don't run from draw contracts; read and understand them before making your final decision, as you would with any of the other pay structures. Like I said, any contract could be good. You need to analyze it to know (LM).

Now that I've outlined the differences among simple production, adjusted production, collections, and a draw, we can dive further into receiving an actual contract offer. I find it's wise never to accept or reject any offer in person unless you're 100% certain you want the job. Let me say that again: unless you WANT the job. If I were you, I'd never decline a job offered at the interview unless you learned something during the interview that made you really not want the job. Speaking for myself, I'd have to see something pretty egregious to decline an offer outright—something along the lines of walking in to meet the owner and finding them doing an RCT without a rubber dam (illegal), sterilization issues in the back (safety concern), or obvious billing fraud.

I'd have no problem mentioning any of these things to the owner. I might say, for example, "I'm sorry, Dr. XYZ, I'm going to have to decline your offer because my number-one goal is safety. I saw you doing an RCT without a rubber dam, and that's illegal as well as unsafe for the patient. I can't work in an environment that encourages illegal or unsafe behavior." This lets them know why you are saying no and sets up a wall: There is no negotiating. This kind of outright decline isn't because the money's not right but because of a true deal-breaker.

Basically, except for reasons such as the ones cited above, I think you should "collect" contract offers early in your career (LM). For one thing, this gives you confidence in your approach; it must be working well if you keep getting offers. Moreover, the more offers you get, the more practice you get reviewing and negotiating the contracts.

I'm not going to kid you. When I first came out of dental school and received all those initial contract offers, I was overwhelmed. I had no idea how to review them effectively or efficiently. As I mentioned, I wasted countless hours on Google just trying to piece together a basic understanding of the contract terminology. If it weren't for my highly competitive nature and my ability to turn the task of contract review into a game, I'm not sure whether I'd have ever fully understood the contracts.

Nowadays, I can read contracts without my Contract Terminology Cheat Sheet and can efficiently review a contract of 5–15 pages in under an hour. This is where you will be after reading this book and working your way through a contract or two. I have past students message me about how they had my terminology cheat sheet pulled up as they worked through their first two contract offers. Now, just like me, they can review a contract without the help of the cheat sheet in less than an hour. Again, practice makes perfect. This is another reason why I recommend getting contracts as soon and as often as possible. You can practice reviewing them, and when you finally receive a contract from an office you're very interested in, you can look it over and respond quickly to the offer.

Another saying that I find rings true in the business of landing a contract is "speed kills." If you can review the contract quickly and respond with either a negotiation, an acceptance, or a rejection within 48 hours, your chances of getting what you want goes up significantly. Speed also helps if the office makes an "exploding offer," which, colleagues have told me, some DSOs are fond of doing. Commonly known as "decaying offers" in other industries, they're designed in such a way that the best possible scenario for the associate is presented on day one and decays daily (or weekly) until it's accepted or expires. For example, on day one the contract offers 35% of collections and a 50% split with the DSO for all lab fees. Day two: 34% of collections and a 50% split. Day three: 34% of collections and the associate pays 60% of the lab fees. Day four: 33% of collections and the associate pays 60% of the lab fees. Day five: 33% of collections and the associate pays 70% of the lab fees. Day six: 32% of collections and the associate pays 70% of the lab fees. Day seven: Offer retracted.

As you can see, the offer gets worse and worse the longer the associate waits to reply. DSOs that use exploding offers are using the psychological principle of urgency. As you'll see in the negotiations section, there are several psychological principles that can be employed during negotiations to try and gain an advantage. No longer will we, however, as associate dentists, fall victim to the psychological ploys of these corporations.

At the end of this chapter, you should have a firm understanding of the three main ways associate dentists are paid: collections, adjusted production, and simple production. If all patient demographics are held constant, then a simple production agreement would likely be best for an associate, but this is often not the case in the real world. Instead, we need to learn how to analyze an agreement. We need to be able to collect financial figures from a possible employer and assess if they are beneficial for you. Only then can you say one contract is better than the other. No more will we hold the common misbelief that collections contracts are bad or that simple production contracts are always good. Because that is just not true (LM). Moving into Chapter 8 we will discuss the actual contract offer and how I approach contract reviews.

Chapter Summary Points:

1. **The three main ways associate dentists are paid include collections, adjusted production, and simple production**
2. **No single pay structure is universally better than the others. Every contract is different. Every contract has the potential to be a great one or a bad one. You must read it and decide for yourself.**
3. **Collections-based contracts can earn you as much or more than production-based contracts depending on practice demographics**
4. **Collect contract offers early in your career by avoiding saying no during the interview**
5. **Avoid falling victim to a decaying offer**

Chapter 8

Associate Agreement Overview

Sitting down to review the first associate dentist contract I ever got was a very exciting moment for me... well, until I realized—very quickly—the language didn't read like my favorite novel. Instead, it was more like my first time studying a foreign language. When it's your turn, you'll see many things you recognize, but the structure and flow will be new to you, especially if you haven't dealt with legal contracts before. For those of you familiar with Christian theology, contracts are more like the Bible. By that I mean they typically don't read front to back, the way a normal book does (LM). They read in sections, and sometimes the first section you should read is on page three, rather than page one as I first thought. I will start this chapter with a very basic overview of what sections are typically found in an associate dentist agreement. That way the contract is no longer an ambiguous document that you know very little about, and you should instead be able to anticipate next sections and moreover what should be found in each section. I will end the chapter with a discussion of my technique when it comes to reviewing an agreement, which should allow you to save lots of money on legal fees.

Most contracts will start with a preamble, which is essentially the title of the agreement, the date, and the names of the parties involved. This tends to be copy and paste/ boilerplate material that is essentially the same between agreements at that office. Sometimes there will be a section that includes some form of recitals and definitions. Recitals are essentially the contract's introduction. Overall, the purpose is to provide a clear and concise summary of the background, context, and purpose of the agreement and to ensure all parties have a shared understanding of the contract. Typically, the recitals section includes the names of the parties, date of the agreement, nature of the relationship between the parties, and any background information that may be needed to help clarify the agreement. Mine have tended to be as ambiguous as something can be.

While many contracts won't have a definitions section, if it does, it typically follows the recitals. This section is used to provide clear and concise definitions of the key terms and phrases used throughout the agreement. The purpose of this section is to ensure that all parties have a shared understanding of the meanings of the terms used in the contract, and to avoid any confusion or misinterpretation, which could lead to disputes or misunderstandings down the road. It may include the definitions of terms such as "Dentist," "Practice," "Compensation," "Benefits," "Termination," "Confidentiality," and other such terms. By providing clear and concise definitions, the contract can ensure that the intentions and expectations of both parties are clearly stated and understood. In the event that there is not a clear definitions section, seek clearly stated definitions within each section of the agreement that the term is first introduced within to avoid ambiguity.

One thing to be on the lookout for within this section is a subsection focusing on "exclusivity." The owner may dictate that you can provide dental services *only* for him or her during the term of your proposed contract. I've also seen this worded as "dental services that 'compete' w/ the business." This can include both work you will be compensated for and pro bono work for a charity event. If you like to attend charitable events or want to moonlight at other offices, be sure to strike this exclusivity clause or add an addendum stating what explicitly you want to do in terms of dental work (LM). Moreover, if you plan to join the lecture circuit, I recommend you make an addendum to this section since the owner may try to restrict your access to all dental-related fields of work. Another way to get things in writing is to send an email that summarizes what you and the owner talked about during any in-person communication. If they don't reply, you still have a record of the meeting. If they do reply, you have both versions in writing should any legal action be taken in the future (LM). Just be aware that most agreements have an "entire agreement" provision, which provides that the agreement document represents the full and complete agreement of the parties and other writings are null and void, which could make your email meaningless in a court of law.

Another important subsection is "the facilities," which is a generalized way of defining where you'll work. Pay attention to the specific address or addresses listed, especially in corporate settings since this is where you may end up working (LM). There should also be a list of all the resources with which they'll be supplying you. I would strongly encourage you to make sure the following sentence is in any agreement you sign: "[XYZ employer] is responsible for providing the associate dentist all necessary equipment and appropriately licensed personnel to effectively complete their job as a dentist in [XYZ state(s)]." (LM) This is essentially a legal promise to get you what you need to do dentistry—operatories, licensed staff, and supplies. Make sure they list everything you will need to be successful. If it isn't listed, you may not have it once you start there. I have heard of an office that didn't have high-speed handpieces. How was an associate supposed to work without a handpiece? Just make sure the list is there. Last note, look for a clause saying you can or cannot bring your own instruments as well as who the property/instruments belong to. Should you decide to bring in your own extra oral camera, you don't want the office now claiming it as theirs.

I've had contracts that included a "Duties and Terms" section next, but I've also seen this section listed later (after compensation). For the sake of simplicity, I'll discuss these sections now. From an overview the duties term, is where I'm most interested in the nondental aspects. For example, a lot of contracts talk about managerial expectations or tell you vaguely you must do administrative work. Are you being compensated in any way for this added task? If not, move to strike these clauses.

Specifically, the duties term is yet another section that focuses on defining your role as an associate dentist. Basically, it lays out how you'll conduct ethical and responsible dentistry while following the law. This section often discusses "infirmity," a physical or mental weakness or ailment that becomes chronic or persistent. By signing, you're agreeing that you'll do anything possible to avoid becoming unable to work. This section often quotes an amount of time, such as five days, by the end of which an employer must give an associate written notification that they won't be allowed to provide dental services at their office until the disability improves. Basically, you can be put on unpaid leave if they find that your health is limiting your dental work. This includes both physical and mental health (LM).

To that end, if you have a long-standing health condition that impacts your ability to work, I recommend being upfront and honest with the employer. My wife, for example, experiences debilitating migraines. They're not all that frequent, but when she gets one, she often gets several over the next 7–10 days. When a migraine strikes, she simply can't work. If, in her first week of work at a new office, she were to have two or three migraines and miss several days of work, her employer would rightfully be concerned. If they didn't know about the migraines in advance, they might even consider letting her go. Over time they'd see that she only misses a handful of workdays a year and that it's really not an issue. The unfortunate timing of migraines in our example aside, recurring illness should be brought up *before* you sign a contract. If you are to be a great fit there long-term, they will need to know about and be able to triage any medical leave situations that might arise with as little strain to both parties as possible. Being upfront and honest is my best advice for a long-term successful relationship with your possible future employer (LM). Lastly, should the employer respond negatively when you bring up your medical condition, at least you found out before you started how they will respond.

For the term section, I'm focusing on the length of the employment, but most importantly the auto-renewal clause is what I'm looking out for specifically. My agreements have requested at least 90 days' notice before the end of my current term to void the auto renewal. If you aren't planning to renew or want to negotiate new terms, set a reminder in your phone calendar to send an email before the date of the auto renewal.

Next, the contract may discuss working facilities, expenses, and benefits. This section is especially important if you're considering filing taxes as a W-2 rather than a 1099 independent contractor. This is one of the sections we will spend ample time negotiating. So, more discussion on this will come in Chapter 10.

At this point we are well into the body of the agreement. It has laid out your proposed "scope of work," which is used to define the responsibilities of the dentist, including what specific services are to be provided and the anticipated quality of those services. Often, the "term of employment" is mentioned in the Termination section, which might also include the office work schedule and any leave requests. I personally prefer "at-will" contracts, which basically means either you or the employer can terminate the relationship at any time as long as a specific duration of notice is provided (often 14 to 90 days). These types of relationships are preferred for new doctors as the enhanced flexibility to leave if you find yourself disliking the position can be worth its weight in gold. In fairness, if a signing or relation bonus is factored into the agreement, then negotiating an at-will contract will be more challenging. More on this in Chapter 10 as well but briefly when you obtain a signing/ relocation bonus you will have paid Federal, Social Security and Medicare taxes on the bonus before the money hits your actual bank account. That means your $10,000 bonus is more like $7,000. If there isn't a clause to protect you and you are terminated shortly after starting it might be challenging for newer associates to find the full $10,000 to pay back your bonus. To that end, consider adding a clause to the agreement to protect yourself. Something along the lines of if you are terminated without cause, you do not owe any portion of the bonus back to them.

Now back to the actual agreement and your proposed work schedule. In truth, most of my contracts did very little to define the schedule or even the term of the employment; rather, they gave a dictionary definition of what these terms meant within the given dental agreement. A contract may say things such as, "The Employee shall work on the schedule that is agreed upon by the employee and employer on <u>Schedule 2.1</u>." To find out what schedule you're agreeing to, you have to flip to <u>Schedule 2.1</u>. This is an example of how your contract doesn't read like a book. It helps to have both a printed and a digital version (LM). I read the paper version and use the computer to search for "<u>schedules</u> or <u>sections</u> to enhance the readability of the contract" on my first pass through it. It's easy to get lost flipping between 25 pages of contract and different schedules/sections.

The final areas of the agreement to discuss in more depth are the Termination section as well as the legal clauses tied to the contract. I always encourage new graduates to have an exit strategy in mind before signing an agreement in the first place. You need to review the Termination section closely. Sometimes, there are clawbacks against bonuses or benefits you already received. To make matters worse, sometimes the clawbacks can be invoked even if the employer terminates you, without cause. So be sure to have a very firm understanding of your noncompete clauses, clawbacks and future work restrictions before signing the agreement (LM).

Most agreements have a section(s) that discuss confidentiality, dispute resolution, governing laws and the final signature(s) and date thus making the document official. Confidentiality means you won't share any company materials, even on-boarding/ training material. Anything the company gives you should be kept private long term. The governing law defines in what state any dispute resolutions would take place and that the document is legally binding and not anything said verbally during conversations. The dispute resolution section normally details the monetary value awarded for various liquidated damages. This always has a lot of nasty language along the lines of "we can't actually calculate what the damages will be so we both agree it is "X." The section also details the Use of Name and non-solicitation of patients and staff.

We have now looked at an associate agreement from an overview perspective. The sections and subsections that are often included should no longer be so mysterious to you. Next, we will discuss how I approach every agreement offered to me; it's a systematized approach that helps make sure I don't miss anything. At the end of the day, you are signing a legal agreement that can be used against you in a court of law. While I didn't personally use an attorney to review any of my agreements out of dental school, if you want more assurance or have any specific questions, then seeking legal counsel is always my advice! (But keep reading—I say more about this in the next section.) However, if you are a DIY person like myself, the next few pages should really help you to analyze an agreement in a systematized fashion. The last thing that I will add is that I only suggest this approach for basic associate agreements and never for practice purchase or partnership agreements, these should always be reviewed by a competent attorney.

<u>Reviewing an Associate Agreement – A Systematized Approach</u>

Now that you've received a contract, we will go through it. My approach requires several independent passes through the entire agreement. Each pass will have a different purpose, and collectively they will work together to decrease the chance that we will miss anything of vital importance. While the approach seems tedious, keep in mind that this agreement could have more impact on your life over the coming months or years than about anything else. So going slowly is always advisable. We will obviously start with pass number one!

Now that you've gotten your first contract, it's time to figure out what exactly the practice is offering you. Print out a copy and just go through it. Go ahead and read it from the first page to the last (even though that may not be the most efficient). On this first pass I want you to gather a very basic understanding of what all is there. There is no need to spend a ton of time on this pass making sure all the clauses and terms are in your best interest; we will do that later. Additionally, try not to get bogged down by difficult terminology.

This first read gives you the opportunity to take in what's there. Poorly written contracts often have several sections discussing pay or benefits. My first contract was an absolute mess. The owners had created 10 different addendum sections where they kept adding to my benefits. The contract would say things like "according to section 3.1 under addendum 2.0, the associate will receive the greater of 30% adjusted production and/or $450 daily guarantee." On a first pass through the agreement, just try to get a grasp of what is being offered in a very general sense.

You are now beginning to understand what exactly the office is offering you. You certainly don't understand the agreement in its entirety, but you have a general concept. If the offer is substantially worse than you were expecting, maybe you can stop there and get back to the owners with an answer of "no" to that contract before you spend tons of time digging into the details. Or maybe you were told the offer would be for 35% collections during the interview, only to see a contract offering just 30% collections. Maybe you use that as a stopgap to inquire why the contract is different from what you were told. If you simply had legal counsel review the agreement for you, then you would have paid them to review an agreement when you would have known the answer to that specific contract was an outright declination since it wasn't the same figure you were told in person. Always read your contract at least once on your own before getting anyone's help (LM).

After your first pass through the agreement, you should do a second and third pass with a pen in hand. These reviews start to dig into the nuanced details of the document while still avoiding getting bogged down in any one topic. On this set of reviews, you should have the Contract Terminology Cheat Sheet pulled up and you should be making notes on your paper version. Just keep gathering an understanding of what's there and note any questions or concerns you see. We will try to understand these questions or concerns in pass number four. The second pass is focused on the financial side of the agreement, while the third pass looks at duties and expectations as well as the remaining legal components.

Specifically for pass number two, I recommend making sure all the relevant details, such as payment schedule(s) and infirmity clauses, are properly outlined. Also, make sure the contract contains any necessary disclaimers and indemnification clauses. Review the general terms and conditions of the agreement and investigate the benefits offered. This is where you should spend some time trying to evaluate for yourself how much each individual benefit means to you. For example, if you have young children, then health insurance may be critical for you, while a single dentist may be more concerned with a signing bonus or student loan repayments. You need to audit the agreement against what you personally need in terms of benefits. Every doctor will want/require different benefits; it's a very personal choice.

For pass number three we will delve into your scope of work, including clinical responsibilities and patient load. Understand how patients—especially new patients—get divvied up. Make sure to understand any productivity expectations. Confirm details regarding schedule, on-call duties, and vacation time. We will also assess the legality of the document by scrutinizing the termination clauses, notice periods, and grounds for contract termination. Be sure to check for clauses related to malpractice insurance, liability, and noncompete clauses. Lastly, review any provisions regarding dispute resolution, confidentiality, or changes to the agreement.

You're probably thinking that you're ready to reply to the owners and start negotiating, but wait. That was only our first three passes through the contract, and we still have at least one more to make sure we don't miss anything. Now we need to dig into the nitty-gritty details of the agreement. At this point you have a decent understanding of the contract after just three passes. You may still be missing some details, which is the purpose of a fourth pass. On this fourth pass/assessment you will pay attention to only the nuances or questions you marked from any of the first three passes. You may still need to look things up on my cheat sheet document or on Google. This pass is the detailed pass where you focus on areas of concern. After this pass, you either fully understand the agreement or possibly have a few lingering concerns. Full understanding means you understand every single word. If you don't have a full understanding, you could reach out to a mentor, reach out to me at TheEducatedAssociate.com, or seek legal guidance from a competent attorney. Below, you will find a very competent attorney I have personally worked with, they are a team of two brothers, Alexander and Michael Besmer, DDS and J.D respectively. Please reach out to them with any final questions or concerns. The good news is, should you seek legal counsel, now you will approach your attorney with a specific question(s) rather than saying, "Hey, here is this document. Can you read it for me?" The financial savings you will experience using this approach can be startling. If you don't already know this, attorneys are paid hourly, and they bill in 6-minute increments. That means the less you give them to do, the less you pay. Moreover, you personally have developed a great understanding of what the contract says. When you understand your contract yourself, things can function much better than if you are taking your legal team's word for it.

At this point, you are fully aware of the intricacies of the agreement and know well what is being offered. You are now informed and ready to improve the agreement with some good old-fashioned negotiation, which we will discuss shortly. But first we will decide whether or not the job being offered is really the one you want. To that end, we will discuss the contract in terms of two main components in my mind, the compensation and benefits offered and the exit strategy.

Last note, the information provided does not and is not intended to constitute legal advice. For counseling services contact:

Alexander Besmer, DDS and Michael Besmer J.D.

(561) 339-9787 or besmerdds@gmail.com

Chapter Summary Points:

1. "At-will contracts are preferred for first associateships.

2. Have a print and a digital version of your contract available for review whenever reading an agreement.

3. Read your contract once without stopping for an overview.

4. Read your contract a second and third time with the Contract Terminology Cheat Sheet pulled up.

5. Read your contract a fourth time to analyze the nitty-gritty details.

6. Seek legal advice on topics you don't fully understand rather than on the entire agreement.

Chapter 9

Deciding if the Office Is Right for You

At this point you have made your way through a slew of online communications with multiple offices, and you have also had several in-person/online interviews where you had the opportunity to directly assess the office, office culture, owner's personality, and see the physical location(s). You have also obtained at least one associate agreement, read it multiple times, and know the ins and outs like the back of your hand. You should have a pretty solid understanding of the office vibe and what kind of benefits they are willing to give you. Now you are ready to decide for yourself if this job being offered is your dream job, a good match, OK, or just plain bad.

This section of the book will have less personal guidance than other chapters, as I feel very strongly that there is no single perfect associateship for everyone. Some doctors are seeking the highest pay possible, while others want work-life balance. Those two offices likely couldn't be more different, so determining a good fit is truly a personal/family decision. I do however have several questions/topics that may help you decide for yourself.

1. What benefits am I getting?

The benefits available to associates are highly variable, although I have noticed a trend toward better benefits at DSOs compared to private offices. In my personal experience, my first associateship paid me on production and also paid about $750 per month toward my student loans. There were no other benefits. No health insurance. No 401(k) or match. Nothing else. This office was of course a private practice. Fortunately, my wife is a pediatrician, and she was working in residency at the time, so our medical benefits came through her hospital and this wasn't an issue for me.

In a later associateship, I had full benefits, one could say. I had the option to obtain health, dental, and vision insurance. The employer paid for my malpractice insurance premiums, and I received $3,000 in CE reimbursement. I had the option for a 401(k) but there wasn't a match. I'm sure there are other benefits I am missing, but you get the gist. This associateship was with a DSO.

While my experience is certainly not universal, there is a trend toward DSOs and better benefit packages. So, if benefits are critical for you, then you may have to take the corporate route initially.

2. Will the compensation structure support me both when I start and long-term? Should I stay for over a year?

As much as we often don't want to talk about budgets and finances, it's very important to approach your future financial situation with a plan. I would encourage you to make a budget and make sure to factor in student loan payments, as that could be new for you. Visit your lender's website as soon as possible to get a feel for what your payments might look like with varying incomes. Obviously, if you won't earn enough long-term to support the life you want, then the job won't work out, but you also need to think on the short-term time scale as well.

When I graduated I had virtually no money left to my name after paying for my dental license, boards, and just living. If you will have to move for the job, that can cost as little as nothing but could go all the way up to $20,000 or more if you are moving across the country with a family. If the associateship you desire is multiple states away, I would really encourage you to seek a moving allowance, stipend, signing bonus, relocation bonus, or any means of obtaining some cash before you need to move. The key word there is *before* you move. On one agreement, my wife (pediatrician) was offered a relocation bonus of $15,000. Little did we know, she got the bonus after starting to work. So basically, it wasn't a true relocation bonus; it was a starting bonus. Well, we had banked on having the money for the move, and that wasn't the case. So, learn from us and make sure you will get the cash well before you plan to move (LM).

3. Exit strategy?

Up to this point, we have aimed at obtaining the best associateship match for you as possible. Reality is that at some point it is very likely you will need to transition out of this associateship. To that end, your agreement needs to be flexible regarding an exit strategy. For many new dentists this means negotiating for small and short noncompetes and at-will contracts. For others, this means avoiding signing bonuses and draw-like contracts so you don't have any financial limitations to leaving. Personally, I think it is very important to analyze your exit strategy before signing the contract. Even silver tarnishes; don't be naive and think your first associateship won't tarnish at some point as well. Think through your exit strategy before signing the agreement, and the future you will be thankful for your foresight.

4. Did I notice any red flags while interviewing?

If you had that feeling in your gut that something was amiss, trust your gut. I would really encourage newer doctors to trust themselves. If you find yourself trying to talk yourself into a job, saying things like "The owner sure seemed like a jerk, but the pay was exceptional," don't think about it—just run. It's not going to be worth it if you find yourself making deals with yourself. Red flags are just that—a sign to run the other direction and never look back.

5. Will the office be able to support me as an additional doctor?

This can be a bit more challenging to answer, but I do have some additional questions you should deploy while interviewing to help you grasp whether the office can actually support you there.

a. How far out into the future is current treatment being booked for the lead doctor, the previous associate, or the other doctors in house? Two to four weeks is a good sign. Much longer or shorter should warrant more investigation.

b. Is the office staff doing their job collecting? Collections rate should be 96% or higher.

c. Current number of active patients? We want at least 1,200 but more likely need 1,500–2,000 active patients to require an associate.

d. Average number of new patients each month? Ideally, 20 or more.

e. How are the new patients divvied up? If you as the associate don't get access to at least half, I would consider that a red flag ▶ .

6. Will I be able to advance my dental skills or treatments I offer while working there?

In my mind the entire point of being an associate out of training is to learn to be a more efficient doctor while not having to worry about the finances or business side of dentistry. If, for example, the office plans to have you knocking out quad after quad of class II resin restorations, you likely won't learn any advanced dental treatments like implant fixture placement. If you look at your entire dental career as a timeline, you will earn far more money in your entire career by learning to do advanced treatments as opposed to simply doing drill-and-fill dentistry your entire career.

That is why I encourage newer doctors to select learning over earning while early out. Simply put, while getting fast and good at resins is important, it shouldn't be your only focus in your first associateship. I would really encourage newer docs to focus on learning advanced skills over making money on simple dentistry early in your career.

7. Will my work schedule negatively impact my ideal work-life balance?

I know that when I was finally done with training, I wanted nothing more than more relaxation in my life. I was sick and tired of the day in, day out grind of dental school. I no longer wanted to dump 80 hours a week into dentistry. I wanted to get back into riding my bike and having nice weekends to have enjoyable experiences with my two young children. I was seeking a balance between work and life for the first time in my life. I knew working from 8:00 a.m. to 5:00 p.m. five days or more a week wasn't for me at that time. I therefore sought out a practice with less working hours than described above. Again, this is very personal, but you will need to decide what kind of balance is right for you and make sure you will have the opportunity for that balance while working there.

8. What is the office policy on treating primary family members, extended family, and friends?

I've noticed that every owner is very different on how they expect you to bill treatments you perform on family members and friends. I had one previous owner make me bill both family and friends at full cost with no discount whatsoever. I never asked him the policy before I did a filling on my friend, and when I planned to do the restoration for free, the owner took the money out of my next paycheck to cover the filling. So not only did I do the filling, but I also got to pay for it. On the other hand, I had another owner who was totally the opposite. Any treatments on primary family members were free other than covering a possible lab bill for indirect restorations. At this office any treatments for friends or extended family were also encouraged but billed at 50% the normal fee. A third owner was between the previous two owners and made me bill all family members at 75% the normal fee.

Long story short, if you plan to do treatments to family or friends, I would get an understanding of the office policy before signing a contract (LM). Even better would be to have the policy in writing as a portion of the agreement.

The owner who charged me for the filling on my friend lost his associate shortly thereafter. The office that encouraged treatments for family members still made a large profit, as my father-in-law ended up having some extensive work done that he elected to pay in full (his choice), as he was pleased with the free work we had done for his wife.

9. How does your commute look?

This question in many ways piggybacks off the question about work-life balance. At my first office I had a 25-minute commute to and from work. Basically, this added an hour of time away from home to my daily routine, which accounted for 5 extra hours a week or 20+ hours in a month. Unlike time where I was in the physical office with an opportunity to earn money, this was unpaid time. Longer commutes also increased my degree of burnout. I would encourage you to find an associateship close to your residence, as this will save you from the financial toils and stress of a long commute.

As mentioned at the start of this chapter, there is no perfect associateship for every dentist. There is, however, a perfect associateship out there for each of us. It just takes time and effort to find the one that is specifically right for you. If you have followed the strategies laid out in this book, you have at least obtained several interviews and hopefully even a handful of associate agreements. You should feel very excited as your dream of becoming a fully functional dentist who works in the community of your choosing is so close that I bet you can taste it. I am also excited for you, but I want to encourage you not to rush through the final steps before starting your first associateship, and make sure you negotiate your agreement to the utmost extent possible. Negotiation is where we make sure the agreement is structured in a way that you want, and like so many things in this chapter, what you want is always a personal choice. So, make sure you know what contract items are most important to you. We will discuss negotiating your agreement in the next chapter!

Chapter Summary Points:

1. **Use the questions listed in the chapter to decide if the associateship being offered is a good fit for you and your family!**

Chapter 10

Negotiating Your Dream Contract

According to Benjamin Franklin, "Failing to prepare is preparing to fail." In dentistry, an Educated Associate needs to be ready to negotiate not just now but every single day of their career. Therefore, the time you spend today enhancing your ability to negotiate will pay dividends both nowadays with your agreement but also long-term with many other aspects of life, such as future car or home purchases.

Frankly put, to get the associate agreement you desire, you need to become a strong negotiator. Believe me, confrontation and negotiation do not come naturally to me. In fact, I mostly do everything I can to avoid confrontation in my everyday life. It's just not my personality, and I have a pistol of a wife who normally does that hard work for us. When it came to my associate agreements, however, it was all on me, and I couldn't lean on my wife. So, I did what I normally do and what you are doing by reading this book: I found an expert source and leaned into it. I started my journey into becoming a master negotiator by reading the book *Never Split the Difference,* by Chris Voss, an ex-FBI hostage negotiator who does an exceptional job of walking his readers through the complex process of negotiation. I will do my best to summarize my version of his breathtaking work while putting my personal spin on it in this chapter. My strategy has worked numerous times for me with associate agreement negotiations as well as in non-professional settings with things like purchasing a new car.

As I alluded to before, failing to prepare is like entering a contract negotiation without a strategy. Having a strategy is how the FBI has saved countless hostage lives and is also how you will negotiate the associate agreement you deserve.

The process of negotiation really starts by fully understanding the agreement, as we discussed in chapter 8. After you fully understood the agreement, you were able to decide if the practice and agreement were right for you in chapter 9. You have had time to think about what is important to you in terms of benefits, compensation, and work-life balance. I would go as far as saying you should rank your desired benefits, compensation, and vacation time in a perfect world setting. It's unlikely we will be able to get everything you want in the agreement, but with a ranked order of what's most important, we can at least ensure we nail the highest priority items first. Now back to negotiation.

First we need to learn how to ask calibrated questions during the interview and negotiation stage(s). One should ask open-ended questions that encourage the other person to provide detailed responses, which can reveal valuable information and help guide the negotiation. In his book, Chris Voss strongly suggests asking questions that start with the word "how." This makes the other person in the negotiation stop and think. It also prevents them from escaping the negotiation by answering with a simple "yes" or "no," one-word answer. When people start answering "how" questions, they often end up providing more information than they had hoped to give away.

By asking the right questions and then actively listening to the answers, you can gain an advantage over the person with whom you are negotiating. Active listening involves paying close attention to the other person's words, tone, and emotions to understand their perspective and build rapport. You must also pay close attention to their body posture, head, eye, and hand movements and look for a "tell." It has been shown that over half of what someone is "saying" is conveyed via nonverbal exchanges such as their mannerisms or degree of eye contact, so be sure to watch them actively and not just listen. Thus, negotiating in person is technically easier than negotiating via electronic communication like email, where these visual aspects can't be assessed directly.

In negotiation, a "tell" refers to a subtle or unintentional signal or clue displayed by the other party that provides insights into their thoughts, intentions, or emotions. These signals can be verbal or nonverbal cues that indicate important information about their position, level of interest, or willingness to make concessions.

Examples of negotiation tells might include a change in tone of voice, body language, facial expressions, hesitation in speech, or certain phrases or words used. By observing and interpreting these tells, negotiators can gain valuable insights into the other party's perspective, emotions, or hidden motivations. This information can then be used to adjust one's approach, ask more targeted questions, or make informed decisions during the negotiation process.

While noticing a tell can be very helpful, it's important to note that tells are not foolproof and should be considered alongside other factors. People may intentionally deceive or mask their true thoughts, so it's crucial to use tells as just one piece of the negotiation puzzle and not rely solely on them.

Other aspects of active listening that can help make negotiations move along include deploying tactical empathy as well as the practice(s) of mirroring and/or labeling to help create a connection and facilitate understanding. Briefly, tactical empathy is the practice of attempting to understand the other person's point of view and emotions, even if you don't agree with them logically. This type of empathy helps build trust and enables you to find mutually beneficial solutions. Mirroring involves reflecting the other person's words or behavior to show that you are listening and to encourage them to continue talking. Labeling is the acknowledgment of the other person's feelings and emotions by using labels such as "It seems like …" or "It sounds like …," which in turn helps create a connection and fosters understanding. The overall purpose of these strategies is to keep the other person talking so that you can uncover a possible "black swan."

In negotiation, a "black swan" refers to an unexpected or highly improbable event or piece of information that has a significant impact on the outcome of the negotiation. The term "black swan" originates from the belief that all swans were white until the discovery of black swans in Australia, which challenged the existing assumption.

In the context of negotiation, a black swan can be a game-changer that disrupts the expected course of the negotiation, introduces new information, or shifts the dynamics in a significant way. It can be a surprising revelation, a previously undisclosed piece of information, an unforeseen external factor, or an alternative solution that hadn't been considered before.

Black swans can either work in favor of one party or create opportunities for mutually beneficial outcomes. They have the potential to break impasses, challenge assumptions, and open up new possibilities for creative problem-solving.

Identifying and leveraging black swans requires careful observation, active listening, and a flexible mindset during the negotiation process. By being open to unexpected information or events, negotiators can adapt their strategies and explore innovative solutions that may not have been apparent before the black swan emerged.

In one of my contract negotiations I learned that the owner had previously had an associate dentist consistently working with him for nearly five years without any break in their time there. The owner had grown accustomed to having an associate in the office. Having an associate allowed the owner to take routine vacations, not work Fridays, and leave early on occasion. Before I applied, the office had gone nearly nine months without an associate dentist. The owner was feeling depressed and was really circling the drain, as he couldn't afford to close the office and go on vacation, was now working five days a week, and was stuck until all patients left every day of the week. His world had flipped upside down on him when the previous associate left. Up until this point in the conversation, all the leverage I thought I had in the negotiation was that I was a dentist who wanted to work in the same geographic area as his office. Upon discovery of this information, a true black swan emerged, and I learned how much leverage I really had. This man needed an associate, and he needed them nine months ago.

In the initial contract negotiation before appreciating this black swan, I had originally asked for a signing bonus of $5,000 and he said no, they couldn't afford it. While I had no idea about their specific financial situation, it no longer mattered in the scheme of the negotiation, as I could now leverage his pain and lack of time off and negotiate with that which was obviously worth way more than $5,000 to him. I then changed my approach and tried a label; "It seems as though you are accustomed to having an associate dentist, and the last nine months without an associate dentist has been very challenging for you and your family. Would you agree?" He replied with "Yes, that is correct." At this point, I had him and could have asked for the same signing bonus or maybe even a higher signing bonus and he would have OK'd it. Instead, I used this new leverage—the black swan—to improve my situation not just that day but for the length of the agreement while also making him think I was still helping him out of his dark situation. I asked for $750 a month of student loan reimbursement for as long as I worked for him. He said yes without hesitation, and we struck a deal we were both happy with.

Two things changed after I learned of the black swan. Obviously, upon appreciating the black swan, I had all the leverage in the negotiation. Secondly, I also learned that he "may not have the money today." This allowed me to change my request slightly, from $5,000 today to a recurring expense of $750/month where he would have time to obtain the capital for the payments. That is why I asked for monthly reimbursement as opposed to a one-time payment. This would allow him to spread the money out over time, which may have helped his financial situation and also made it seem like I would be there earning money for the office, which would certainly offset the student loan reimbursement expense. Learning this black swan helped me to get the associate agreement I wanted while also changing my compensation from a $5,000 signing bonus to $9,000/year of student loan reimbursements. I worked that contract for nearly two years. So, by the end of the contract, my ability to detect his black swan resulted in nearly $18,000 of student loan reimbursement instead of a measly $5,000 at the onset. It was a win for me, and the owner got an associate and was able to start taking some time off again. I think everyone ended up happy with this deal.

As a summary, the negotiation strategy that works best as described in the book *Never Split the Difference* is to ask calibrated questions while actively listening and watching for tells. Deploy a combination of tactical empathy with labeling and mirroring in an attempt to detect a black swan. Then use this critical piece of information to sway the negotiation in your favor. Next, we will explore what portions of an associate agreement tend to be the most negotiable, from my experience.

Technically, everything in an associate agreement is negotiable, but from my experience, there are certain aspects owners tend to be more likely to change while other sections are virtually set in stone. While the personal example above resulted in a reoccurring expense for this owner, in general corporations tend to look to decrease recurring expenses, such as your monthly paycheck or monthly student loan reimbursements. They will, however, be more open to negotiating one-time expenses. There are two main reasons. Number one: tax benefits. More than likely, a lump-sum payment to you or your student loans can be used as a deduction (write-off) against the corporation's yearly taxes. Thus, it tends to be easier to negotiate a signing/relocation bonus as opposed to monthly student loan repayment. However, my personal example showcases how you can also negotiate a reoccurring expense. I suggest you paint the picture for the owner by suggesting that the one-time payment you're seeking will allow them to decrease their tax burden while getting you the money needed to sign the contract. It's a true win-win. The second reason you should negotiate one-time settlements is to "align your goals with those of the practice." I recommend setting up these one-time settlements as an incentive for hitting some of the goals of the office. Aside from producing—and thereby earning the practice as much money as possible—you could tether this increased pay to a less production-based item.

For example, the first office I worked for provided Invisalign clear-aligner therapy. Invisalign has a built-in, ratcheting incentive program. Offices that start 15 new cases every six months get to decrease the cost of producing the aligners by a few hundred dollars per case. If 30 cases are started, an even bigger discount is applied, and so on. You could, therefore, add a clause to your agreement that states "If the office hits the Invisalign goal of 15 cases in my first six months at the office, then I receive a $2,000 bonus, regardless of who starts the cases." This tethers the overall office goal to an item they can measure. By showing you can make the office more profitable while also aligning your goals to theirs, you're not only ensuring you earn more money but also establishing a goal-oriented, goal-aligned relationship before you even step into the clinic. This is another easy way to sway the owner on this type of agreement. If you don't hit the goal, they pay you nothing, and if you do hit the goal, everybody wins.

A final element that has helped me in negotiations is the idea of anchoring. The concept of anchoring is straightforward—it means making the first offer or suggesting an extreme position to set a reference point for the negotiation. This can influence the other person's perception of what is reasonable. For example, if an office wants to pay you on adjusted production and there has been no discussion of the actual percentage, I will place my anchor on the extreme end of the pay spectrum for the geographic region. If for example the average associate gets 28-32% production in your city, I would place my anchor on the upper end of the spectrum when asked what pay rate seems reasonable to me. I would say, "I am expecting between 32-35% adjusted production." This anchor sets the stage for the negotiations; they are unlikely to pay you above the normal rate, but this anchor makes it clear that you will take no less than 32%. From my experience, a properly placed anchor is the best way to dramatically increase your pay rate with minimal effort (LM).

I will end this chapter with a discussion of how I have and would negotiate several specific aspects of an associate agreement such as 1099 vs. W-2, lab fee deductions, bonuses, a daily guarantee, all radiographs billed under yourself, an at-will contract, and as small/short of a noncompete clause as possible, as well as maximizing your continuing education (CE) reimbursement. The overall approach described at the start of the chapter is what you should deploy to negotiate a larger compensation package as a whole. These are the details that will increase your total compensation package.

<u>Negotiating Specific Contract Nuances:</u>

<u>Negotiating a 1099 vs. a W-2 Contract Structure</u>

I'll start this section with an opinion: No associate dentist should be compensated as a 1099. For starters, 1099 implies a contractor and not a full-time employee. Full-time employees should also receive alternative benefits such as health insurance or possibly investment opportunities, such as a 401(k), that are not available to contracted workers. Additionally, as a 1099 you become responsible for both parts of the Medicare and Social Security taxes instead of splitting those taxes with the employer, as a W-2 employee would. The single advantage of being a 1099 is the ability to itemize your tax return more readily, which in some cases could be a financial benefit. One dentist I worked with was a 1099 for three years at two different practices. He said his tax savings on the return were a wash after three years with the increased Medicare and Social Security taxes. Basically, he spent tons of time keeping records of any taxable event so he could itemize, which resulted in no gain and he spent more time and energy. As dentists we need to be buying our time back, not finding ways to waste it. I now universally recommend against a general dentist who works as a full-time associate in a particular office or corporation being hired as a 1099 independent contractor.

Moreover, a major shift has been happening with associate dentists, and that is for employers to pay us as employees but offer no benefits. I have worked at an office as a W-2 employee. In this contract, I was not offered health insurance, 401(k) or 401(k) match, or other benefits. Fortunately, my wife received those benefits through her employer, so it didn't impact me negatively in the long haul, but the missed opportunity still doesn't seem right to me. The more I talk with other associates, the more I find this to be commonplace, especially in private offices.

I am no longer willing to sign agreements that don't offer benefits. I have made it my goal to now negotiate whatever benefits I can into an agreement. At a minimum you should use the strategies from this chapter to negotiate a 401(k) and/or health insurance into every agreement you sign. If you don't need these benefits, they should pay you more. To that end, I would negotiate an overall compensation package and talk about it in dollars and cents. In the bonuses chapter of the book, you will find a formula that you can use to derive a total compensation value that can then be used for more direct monetary comparisons of various offers you receive by also factoring in benefits.

For example, you want to earn $150,000/year while also hitting your 401(k) contribution limit for 2024, $23,000. That would mean you earned $173,000 as an aggregate. You could negotiate with the employer that they either guarantee you a salary of $173,000 or they pay you the $150,000 base and have a benefit where they will match your 401(k) contributions up to 5%. This way you can ensure you are hitting your overall goal but giving the owner a chance to decide what is also best for them. Again, this concept is based around an overall/ total compensation package, which is really how I think you should view your agreement.

<u>Lab fee deductions:</u>

Never sign an agreement with a lab fee deduction greater than your percentage of pay. If you get paid 30% adjusted production, then your lab fee deduction should be 30% of the total fee or less. I frankly tell employers I won't be responsible for more of the lab fee than they are willing to pay me. It has worked every time. In rural environments, you should be able to negotiate no lab fee deductions routinely. Of note, be very careful when evaluating the fees associate with clear aligners like Invisalign. I'm seeing lots of offices splitting lab fees on fixed/ removable prosthodontics but having the associate pay the entire aligner lab fee. The fee for Invisalign can be in the thousands per case, so this is almost certainly a poor deal for an associate to make.

<u>Bonuses:</u>

As alluded to above, bonuses can easily be negotiated into your agreement when you uncover a black swan. I typically negotiate one-time bonuses like a signing bonus or a bonus tied to a specific practice metric. One-time payments are tax deductions for the corporation, and you can sell it to them as a way to get you on board while simultaneously decreasing their yearly tax burden.

To leverage your chances of getting a bonus built into your agreement, talk with the owner/ corporation about aligning your bonus with a current practice goal. As more offices offer clear aligner therapy with the common ratcheting incentive program within these clear aligner manufacturers, I like to tether my bonus to hitting office-wide clear aligner goals. That is an easy sell to an owner who knows the benefits to the entire practice if you can push them to the next level of the ratcheting program. It also makes you look like a real team player since you are trying to align yourself to practice goals before you even start there. It's also a great clinical skill for you to learn and master, so taking on clear aligner cases, decreasing the practice's cost per case, and hitting a bonus are all nice ways to come to an agreement. Yes, agreement had a double meaning there!

<u>Daily guarantee:</u>

As a newer dentist, having a guarantee will allow you to sleep easier at night. When you first start out, you have no patients who know or trust you and therefore no guaranteed income if your pay is 100% collection- or production-based. You do, however, have guaranteed expenses like your student loans. So having a daily guarantee can really make your transition into the practice much better. Many offices will offer a guarantee for your first 30–90 days, but it is on the rare side for a guarantee to last much longer than that.

Frankly, owners will tell you that in a three-month window you should become successful there or you are unlikely to ever be successful there . That is simply untrue. I have found that it typically takes two exchanges with a patient for them to start trusting me. Most patients in practice are seen twice a year at their biannual cleaning appointments. That means that it will take 6–12 months for patients in the office to recognize you and likely trust you as well. I use this as my argument for at least 6 months of a guarantee, but I always aim for 12 months. I tend to place an anchor at 12 months after providing the aforementioned reasoning.

From my experience, they won't go for 12 months, but they will compromise and meet you at 6 months most of the time. The guaranteed pay for 6 months will make your initial start at the practice much less stressful. In 6 months you should be able to drum up enough work to produce routinely.

<u>Radiographs billed under you:</u>

Most initial contracts will either pay you for radiographs done on "your side" (i.e., not from a hygiene check) or for no radiographs whatsoever. Radiographs are a zero-overhead procedure, and owners/corporations are getting sneaky by siphoning off procedures like these to pay themselves. If the radiographs through hygiene checks are not under my production or collections contractually, my negotiation technique is to ask who is legally responsible to read the radiographs. In 100% of U.S. states, it is the dentist's job only. Therefore, you should be paid for 100% of the radiographs you read, whether through hygiene or your side. If you do an exam after a hygiene appointment, make sure you are paid for that. In many cases, just being compensated for all radiographs will boost your weekly production by $1,000 or more! In a full year, we are talking about thousands of dollars of possible income in your pocket. As my dad would say, "don't let that loose change get away from you".

From the owner's perspective, they often say things like "the hygienist is being paid for those radiographs because he or she made them." I always chuckle because I haven't yet met a hygienist who was actually paid on production or collections; they are almost universally paid an hourly rate. The hygienist is simply not being paid for those radiographs. That's a lying owner—be cautious.

<u>At-will contract:</u>

Up to this point the entire book has been aimed at getting you into your dream associateship. Reality is that your first associateship is unlikely to be your only job/ associateship you will work in your career. As time goes on you will grow as a clinician and more than likely you will outgrow that office at some point. To that end, your contract shouldn't have a specific length. You and the owner should lay out a reasonable duration of notice for termination of the associate agreement. I suggest 30 days as a reasonable starting point. All this means is that if you or the owner doesn't feel like the relationship is working out, all either of you has to do is give the other party notice of the termination 30 days before you are done working there. I think this clause really protects both parties, and I always bring it up as a mutually beneficial solution to a workplace relationship!

In some cases when the employer is giving you a signing bonus, they will tie that bonus to a length of time you will have to work there or you have to pay back some or all of the initial bonus. That is why I aim for relocation bonuses rather than signing bonuses personally, but their point is valid. If they give you a signing bonus, they do expect a duration of time you owe them. When you obtain a signing bonus, you pay taxes on it before you even receive it. So that $10,000 bonus is more like $6,500 that will actually hit your checking account. Here is the catch: If you leave the associateship early they will seek the full $10,000, which you never really had in the first place. The only work-around is to deploy the signing bonus in a high-yield savings account as soon as you have it. These accounts predictably earn 2-5% interest rates on the balance. Therefore, depending on when you want to leave the associateship, maybe some of the money that was lost to taxes initially has been recouped by the interest you earned. No matter what, you will likely need other finances to get that $10,000 back to them to leave early. And yes, if you are wondering if a corporation will come after that $10,000, you can bet everything you own that they will. Whether that's to prove a point or to get the money, they will do it in every circumstance. You are far better off playing it safe, and if/when you decide to leave the practice, I would give my resignation letter in writing with a check for $10,000 or whatever prorated portion of the initial bonus you will owe them. That sets the record straight right from the start and you will be free to leave. Maintain your reputation and move on to better things.

<u>Short/small noncompete:</u>

This may be the most highly debated item in any associate agreement. You will hear pundits or possibly even mentors say things like "noncompetes are illegal and are never enforceable" or something along those lines. This is untrue, as there are court-documented cases in which the noncompete was upheld and the dentist had to pay the corporation back. While litigation around this remains a hot topic, don't rely on possibilities, and build your agreement in a way that fully removes the noncompete, which is incredibly unlikely, or at a minimum makes it as small and short as possible.

To that end, there are two main components to a typical associate noncompete, a geographic radius and a time duration. It is critical to negotiate both items to the fullest extent possible. The first thing to evaluate, especially in DSOs or multi-practice companies, is whether the geographic radius is defined around only places where you provide dental services or around every single one of their offices (LM). You need to ensure the agreement is specific only to locations where you bill dental services. Some DSOs have hundreds of offices, and if you have a 3-mile noncompete around every single one of those offices, then it may be extraordinarily challenging to find work in the future. So first and foremost, make sure the agreement is only for practices where you bill.

Next, we want to reduce the time frame more than the radius. If we can get the time frame down to six months or less, then in an absolutely worst-case scenario you quit, don't work anywhere for six months, but then are free to work anywhere you please. On the other hand, a smaller radius but for a much longer time period could in theory preclude you from work for a much longer time period. I prefer the safeguard of knowing that no matter what, I could work wherever I want in half a year.

To facilitate this, I always state my opinion that noncompetes are unlikely to be upheld and if they are upheld the longest they are routinely upheld is for six months, so let's just make that the agreement right from the start and avoid possible litigation in the future for both of us. Again, presenting it as a mutually beneficial solution to a problem while maintaining the security they are seeking from the noncompete. If they don't go for the short time, press into the radius. In most rural areas the radius will be larger than urban. In urban areas seek half the radius they initially recommended. If they ask for 5 miles, negotiate for 2 miles and state how many practices fall in that 2-mile radius. Sometimes when they hear the surprisingly large number of offices they are already precluding you from, they become more amenable to the radius reduction.

At the end of the day, seek to strike the noncompete clause, but that is unlikely to happen. Instead shorten the duration as much as possible first, and go for smaller radius as the final approach.

<u>CE reimbursement:</u>

When I want to obtain CE reimbursement or increase the amount of CE reimbursement they are offering, I ask if they have ever had an associate doing advanced treatments in their office, such as implants, full-mouth rehabilitations, or dental sleep medicine. Typically, they haven't had someone do that. I then ask what they think it would mean to the patients if they could now obtain those services in the owner's office. Normally this is exciting, especially if they don't already have those services in house. I am well versed on the additional income that can be generated from these specialized services, and I allude to the increased office production if these services are incorporated in their office.

This is where you bring up doing the CE course with the owner if it's a smaller office. Normally, the owner wants to advance their skill set, and the idea of learning with a colleague is always better than doing it alone. I have personally gotten an owner to pay to fly us both to Las Vegas, where we did a two-day implant seminar. I sold it to him as an excellent opportunity to learn while also having a small vacation. He was thrilled and jumped right on it. He and I had an awesome trip, and we both came back ready to bring implants into the office. We did several implants over the coming month and increased production so much that the trip was paid off in one month's time! I now use this example when talking with future owners about the possibility of learning and increasing production in such a short time period. It was really a win-win. I would encourage you to find a way to make it seem like the owner will get something more than you learning a skill from the CE reimbursement!

At this point Benjamin Franklin would be very proud of you as you are prepared to negotiate your associate agreement. You are ready to ask open ended questions and listen actively for possible tells. You will utilize mirrors and labels to better understand the other party and if you are lucky enough to uncover a Black Swan you will use that to your advantage in an ethical way. We discussed actual strategies to negotiate specific details into your associate agreement. Next, we will discuss signing your agreement and things to consider before your actual start date.

Chapter Summary Points:

1. Read the book *Never Split the Difference*

2. Use a combination of calibrated questions, active listening, and tactical empathy to detect a tell

3. Use labels and mirrors to uncover black swans

4. Leverage black swans to close negotiations in your favor

5. Use your knowledge of associate agreements to negotiate one-time bonuses, increase your options for benefits, and maintain lab fees at reasonable rates

Chapter 11

Signing the Contract and Time Before the Start Date

Once you have negotiated the contract and signed something you are happy with, it's time to get ready for your start date. If you are graduating from dental school, you may still have a few tasks to complete in order to practice in the USA. We will discuss these next steps briefly below. If you already graduated or completed a residency then steps 1-5 below may not be of much value to you. Consider skipping ahead to point #6.

1. **INBDE (Integrated National Board Dental Examination) vs. National Board Dental Examinations (NBDE):**

   a. In previous years, dental students needed to pass the NBDE Part I and Part II exams. Those were the exams I took, and they were scheduled several years apart while in dental school. Nowadays the multi-test scheme of years past has been streamlined to one exam, the INBDE. Passing this two-day exam is required for licensing in most states. Most students take this in their D4 year.

2. **Regional Clinical Board Exams:**

   a. Depending on your future state of desired practice, dentists need to pass a clinical examination: CDCA-WREB, CRDTS, CITA, or SRTA exam(s). The exams are offered in two formats. The traditional format allows for all sections of the exam to be taken over two to three days for students who have already graduated or are soon to graduate. The alternative approach, called the Curriculum Integrated Format (CIF), allows students to complete the exam in sections spread out over their final year of dental school.

b. Use the ADA website to learn more about specific nuances for each state. By that I mean there are five portions of these exams: Restorative, Endodontics, Fixed Prosthodontics, Periodontics, and Diagnostic Skills Examination (DSE). You can take all portions or selected portions based on what may be required by your future state of practice. I encourage all students to take all five components even if the state they currently plan to practice in doesn't require it. The reason is that you will be covered in more states by taking and passing all parts so you will have geographic freedom should that first associateship not work out long-term. You don't want to be doing a new board exam in two years because you are now moving to Florida, and you need the Fixed Prosthodontics section now in Florida when you didn't need it for North Dakota initially. Just take and pass all five sections and move on with your life (LM)!

c. **Just FYI: Delaware** has its own state exam, and **New York** will require a residency to obtain a state dental license.

3. NPI and DEA Registration(s):

In order to prescribe medications, you will need to obtain an NPI and DEA license/numbers. To apply for an NPI (National Provider Identifier) and a DEA (Drug Enforcement Administration) number as a recently graduated dentist, follow these general steps:

a. **National Provider Identifier (NPI) Number:**

i.   Online Application: Visit the National Plan and Provider Enumeration System (NPPES) website and complete the online application for an NPI number.

ii. Personal Information: You will need to provide personal information, including your name, contact details, and other identifying information.

iii. Practice Information: You'll also need to provide information about your practice, including your taxonomy code, which specifies your specialty or area of practice.

iv. Submit Application: After completing the application, submit it through the NPPES website. You will receive your NPI number once the application is processed.

v.   Record Keeping: Keep a record of your NPI number for future reference and use in your practice.

vi. Your NPI number doesn't expire or renew; you just have to update your practice location(s) should you change associateships in the future (LM).

b. **Drug Enforcement Administration (DEA) Registration:**

i.   Application Form: Obtain the DEA registration application form from the DEA website or by contacting the DEA Registration Call Center.

ii. Complete the Form: Fill out the application form with accurate personal and professional information.

iii. Submit Required Documents: Along with the application form, you may need to submit additional documents, such as proof of identity, state license, and other supporting documents as required by the DEA.

    iv.   Fee Payment: Pay the $888 fee for the DEA registration. The fee is due every three years.

    v.   Receive DEA Number: Once your application is processed and approved, you will receive your DEA registration number.

c. Remember that the specific requirements and processes for obtaining an NPI and DEA number can vary by location and individual circumstances. It's advisable to consult the NPI Enumerator and the DEA Registration Call Center for the most accurate and up-to-date information and assistance with the application processes.

4. **CPR, BLS, ACLS, or PALS:** Cardiopulmonary Resuscitation, Basic Life Support, Advanced Cardiovascular Life Support and Pediatric Advanced Life Support

a. In order for a dentist to obtain a state license, they need to maintain at a minimum an active CPR or BLS certification through a registered provider/service. Providers seeking permits for sedation may be required to have further evidence of their safety, such as ACLS (Advanced Cardiopulmonary Life Support) or the children's version, PALS (Pediatric Advanced Life Support). I did my own BLS course for under $200, it renews every two years.

5. **State Licensing:**

a. Apply for a dental license in the state where you intend to practice. Each state has its own licensing requirements, which may include additional exams or documentation. For example, a number of states will require a jurisprudence examination that they create and have you take online after first making another payment for the exam. Not every state but most states do require a nitrous permit if you plan to do nitrous oxide in your future practice.

b. Lastly, gathering a list of character references can be helpful, as some states want character references that are actually from dentists. So maybe consider some of your dental school professors for these references. You should use ADA.org to research specific nuances for your future state of practice. I found it helpful to call the state dental board and make sure I had a firm understanding of everything I was to submit and in what order. This made sure my licenses were processed as quickly as possible (LM).

6. **Obtain Malpractice Insurance:**

a. Secure malpractice or professional liability insurance, especially if it is not provided by your employer.

b. Dentists typically have access to three primary types of malpractice insurance:

i. <u>Occurrence-Based Coverage:</u> This type of insurance covers any incident that occurs during the policy period, regardless of when a claim is filed. Even if a claim is made after the policy has expired, the incident is still covered if it occurred during the policy period. This type of coverage should be preferred by dentists (LM).

ii. <u>Claims-Made Coverage:</u> This insurance covers claims made while the policy is in effect. If a claim is made after the policy expires, there is no coverage, unless the dentist has purchased "tail" coverage or "prior acts" coverage, which extends the reporting period for claims. These tend to have cheaper premiums than occurrence-based, but the cost of the tail makes them costly in the long run.

iii. <u>Malpractice Tail Coverage:</u> Also known as an extended reporting endorsement, this coverage is important for dentists who switch from a claims-made policy to an occurrence-based policy or when leaving a practice. It provides coverage for claims made after the policy has expired for incidents that occurred while the policy was in effect.

c. Each of these types of malpractice insurance offers different advantages and considerations. Clearly, when possible, a dentist should select for an occurrence-based policy. If your employer is planning to pay for your malpractice insurance but will only offer a claims-based policy, I would encourage you to negotiate the occurrence-based option into your contract or see if they will pay the cost of the claims-based policy toward an occurrence-based policy you set up for yourself.

d. Typically, these policies run a new dentist between $800–$2,500/year depending on the types of treatments you provide and any prior history of claims against you.

7. Credentialing:

a. This is the process of setting up your contract with an insurance carrier to provide dental services to their patients. Basically, this is an insurance company OK'ing you to work on their patients and for you to then seek reimbursement from them. Depending on the insurance company, this can take a few days up to several months. Some of the bigger companies, take the longest, so as soon as you know where you plan to work, have the office start credentialing you with their insurance carriers (LM).

8. Visa and Work Authorization:

    a. If you are not a U.S. citizen or permanent resident, then you will need to secure the appropriate visa or work authorization to practice in the USA. This didn't apply to me, so I do not have much advice on this topic.

9. Optional Additional Education:

    a. Some dentists may choose to pursue additional education or specialization once in the USA, such as a residency or advanced degree. I also had classmates take on some CE courses before starting their first job. My first office was in New Mexico. It took 45 days after graduating and submitting my application (which was mistake free) to obtain a license in New Mexico. You could use those 45 days to complete some CE and enhance your clinical acumen.

    b. The office in New Mexico wanted me to show up as an Invisalign provider; they therefore paid for me to take the Invisalign training. I gathered a handful of CE credits, killed some dead time in the mornings during that 45-day waiting period by doing the training, and showed up to work with another tool in my toolbelt.

    c. If you think you will be bored or if the office offers clear aligners, then a quick CE course may be a smart choice with your time before starting work.

It's important to note that the exact requirements can vary by state, so it's always advisable to check with the specific state's dental board for the most accurate and up-to-date information.

At the end of the day, once you have graduated dental school/residency, passed the INBDE and the regional boards, obtained both NPI and DEA numbers, and applied for state licensure, it's time to do something that YOU want to do. You just completed what was likely four or more of the hardest years of your life with very little time to focus on yourself or loved ones. It's now time to refocus your life. If you haven't taken a vacation in years, consider dusting off those old suitcases and hitting a beach somewhere. If you are just worn out, maybe consider a week on the couch binge watching your favorite TV shows. For me, I hadn't physically worked out routinely in years. I purchased a new mountain bike and started to hit the open road with my free time.

I enjoyed pulling my two-year-old daughter in a carriage behind my new bike, and the evaporation of the dad body I had developed in school was an excellent side effect. The fresh air, lack of responsibilities, and tremendous sense of success from completing school all made these rides more rewarding each and every day. I was truly healing my body, heart, and mind after years of abuse.

An often-overlooked aspect of the work-life continuum is your mental health (LM). I never would have guessed how much those simple bike rides improved my mental health. Make time for activities you enjoy, and don't neglect self-care. Taking care of yourself ultimately allows you to provide the best care for your patients.

What you need will be specific to you and your families' circumstances. I know for many of us dental school means little or no ability to focus on our loved ones. I missed out on family event after family event while in school. Consider making a trip to see family if it has been a while since you last made an appearance. It's all about starting to do the things you were forced to put off for years.

For me, this meant being more present with my immediate and extended family. School was such a busy experience that even calling my mom once a week became challenging for me. Sadly, my parents never went to professional school and therefore the rigors of school are often foreign to them. I could tell how much it weighed on my mom that I barely called her anymore. While she understood it was for a "good reason" she was still sad about our relationship. When school ended, I vowed to myself to never go a full week without speaking to my mom again. Nowadays, I talk with my mom on the phone or in person several times a week. Our relationship will likely always have marks from the years I was in school, but we are rekindling the old relationship and I love it!

If possible, I would suggest you reach out to all the family members you feel suffered from you being in school/training. Thank them and let them know you recognize what they did to allow for you to go to school. I haven't met a single dentist who did everything all on their own. Whether it's your parents, significant other, sibling, extended family member, or friend, someone helped you. So, recognize them and let them know you care about them. Often the first step in improving a relationship is to recognize the other person in the relationship. Fixing relationships with those you care about will always be worth it in the long run.

My final piece of advice from this chapter is to take some time before graduating and reflect on what you need to do with your time off. Create a plan and ensure you address your mental, physical, and emotional health. Once you start working, it will be full speed ahead, so use this time carefully!

Chapter Summary Points:

1. **Pass INBDE and clinical exams**

2. **Obtain NPI and DEA license number(s)**

3. **Obtain state dental license(s)**

4. **Obtain malpractice insurance**

5. **Undergo self-reflection to see what you can do to improve your mental, physical, or emotional well-being**

Chapter 12

Insurance in Dentistry

<u>Comparing PPO, HMO, and Medicaid Dental Insurance Plans</u>

When I graduated from dental school my understanding of dental insurance was so simple that I thought insurance plans were there to play a role in helping individuals access affordable dental care. I had no understanding of what the differences or similarities in a PPO, HMO, and Medicaid plans even meant. When I entered practice, I quickly learned that understanding the similarities and differences between various plan types is essential for The Educated Associate to be successful in their career. Understanding insurance will not only make you a better clinician, but it will also improve your earnings in an insurance-based practice. So continue reading if you want to earn more money in your career.

It is always my personal goal to provide value in advance. If this book has provided you actionable advice I'd love to hear from you. You can leave a review on my website, TheEducatedAssociate.com. I'm also looking for topics that you find interesting or would love to learn more about, so please reach out to me on my website or on any social media profile with topics that you want to hear more about. Lastly, if you don't feel like learning insurance today would be beneficial to you, then skip the chapter for now but keep it bookmarked for future use as it will be helpful when you start your job!

In this chapter, we will explore the main features, benefits, and limitations of Preferred Provider Organization (PPO), Health Maintenance Organization (HMO), and Medicaid dental insurance plans. By examining these plan types, I aim to provide a comprehensive understanding of how they function and how they impact dental practices and patients. I am by no means an insurance expert, so there could be some minor mistakes in my attempt to provide a simplified view of an ever increasingly complex subject. If you ever have an insurance-based concern, you should call the insurance carrier for clarity.

<u>PPO, HMO, and Medicaid Differences and Similarities:</u>

1. Preferred Provider Organization (PPO) Plans:
   a. Definition and Characteristics: PPO plans offer a network of preferred dentists who agree to provide dental services at negotiated rates. Patients have the freedom to choose both in-network and out-of-network dentists, but they typically pay less when using in-network providers.
   b. Benefits and Limitations: PPO plans offer flexibility in choosing dentists and usually cover a wide range of dental procedures. However, patients may have higher out-of-pocket costs for out-of-network services, and there may be annual deductibles and waiting periods.

      i. It's important to note that specific plan offerings may vary depending on the geographical location and market. Additionally, each PPO plan may have its own specific coverage details, copayments, deductibles, and limitations. It's always recommended to review the details of the specific PPO plan you are considering or working with to understand its coverage and network.

   c. Finances
      i. From the viewpoint of a dental practice owner, the reimbursement rates between PPO and HMO dental plans can vary significantly. Here are some key considerations:

1. Overview

   (a) PPO Reimbursement Rates:

   (i) Negotiated fees: PPO plans typically involve negotiated fee schedules between the dental practice and the insurance provider. These negotiated fees are often higher than the fees or payments set by HMO plans.

   1. Fee-for-service model: PPO plans generally operate on a fee-for-service basis, where the dental practice bills the insurance company directly for each service provided. The reimbursement rates are based on the agreed-upon fee schedule, which may vary depending on the insurance company and the specific plan.

   (b) HMO Reimbursement Rates:

   (i) Capitated payments: HMO plans usually involve capitated payments, where the dental practice receives a fixed monthly payment per enrolled patient, regardless of the services rendered. This payment is often lower than what would be received for the same services under a PPO plan.

   1. Limited fee negotiation: HMO plans may have limited or no fee negotiation options for individual services. Instead, the dental practice agrees to accept the predetermined fees established by the HMO plan.

   (ii) It's important to note that reimbursement rates can vary widely depending on the specific PPO or HMO plan, the geographic location, and the dental practice's negotiation skills. Additionally, reimbursement rates may differ for different procedures and services within each plan.

(iii) From a financial perspective, dental practices may prefer higher reimbursement rates offered by PPO plans, as they have more flexibility in setting their fees and potentially earn a greater revenue per service. However, HMO plans can provide a steady, predictable patient base with a fixed monthly payment, which may be advantageous for maintaining a consistent cash flow.

2. Health Maintenance Organization (HMO) Plans:

   a. Definition and Characteristics: HMO plans operate on a managed care model, where patients must choose a primary care dentist from a network of providers. Referrals from the primary care dentist are required for specialist visits and certain treatments.

   b. Benefits and Limitations: HMO plans often have lower monthly premiums and predictable copayments. They emphasize preventive care and may have a limited network of dentists. Patients may experience restrictions on choosing providers and navigating the referral process.

3. Medicaid Dental Insurance Plans:

   a. Definition and Characteristics: Medicaid is a government-funded program that provides healthcare coverage to low-income individuals. Medicaid dental plans vary by state but typically cover basic dental services, such as preventive care, restorative procedures, and emergency treatments.

b. Benefits and Limitations: Medicaid plans help individuals who may not have access to other forms of insurance. They offer affordable or no-cost coverage for eligible services. However, limited provider networks, potential delays in accessing care, and coverage limitations for certain procedures may be encountered.

4. Similarities among the plans:

a. Coverage of Preventive Services: PPOs, HMOs, and Medicaid plans generally emphasize preventive care, including regular checkups, cleanings, and X-rays, to maintain optimal oral health.

b. Policy Limitations: All three plan types may impose limitations on coverage, such as waiting periods, annual maximums, and exclusions for certain procedures or pre-existing conditions.

c. Cost-Sharing: Patients often share the cost of dental services in all plan types, whether through copayments, coinsurance, or deductibles.

<u>Dr. Schick's Opinion:</u>

While insurance is a needed service for many of our patients, it becomes one of the most frustrating aspects of our careers as dentists. From a very basic perspective, PPO plans tend to reimburse better than HMO and Medicaid plans. That has sure been my experience. The first office I worked at was well over 50% Medicaid insurance-based patients. It was difficult for me to be profitable with Medicaid reimbursement rates as a new graduate and my slow operating speed initially. For example, a three-surface posterior resin would reimburse around $100, so a quad of teeth would be like $300 and would take me 2 hours when I first started out; I was making $45/hour. My third office is primarily a fee-for-service (FFS) office that accepts one or two PPO plans as well. I do significantly less dentistry and earn more money than I did at my first office. Sometimes it's not about working harder—it's about working smarter. You can potentially leverage the level of insurance and what types of insurance are accepted in your future office to your benefit.

I don't want you to think of insurance as an all-bad thing. In fact, my wife and I were on Medicaid insurance for a few years while in school and with the birth of our daughter. It was extremely helpful and certainly improved our access to care. We were lucky to have some great doctors.

In my mind the key to success in a heavily insurance-based office—especially in one with lower reimbursing insurance carriers—is to become efficient. I'm not encouraging subpar work. I'm saying learn to be as efficient as possible. Learn to prepare the quadrant of teeth in 20 minutes or less, and go do a hygiene exam while the assistant places the interproximal matrix system of your choosing. Come back and restore the quad in 20 minutes or less. Now spend 5 minutes adjusting the occlusion and giving post-operative instructions. When you factor in 10 or so minutes of anesthesia time, you now knocked out a quad and a hygiene exam in just around an hour! You can now be profitable in that insurance setting. It will take time and really just repetition, but you will get there if you keep your mind on it.

Understanding the main similarities and differences between PPO, HMO, and Medicaid dental insurance plans is crucial for dental professionals and patients alike. PPO plans offer flexibility in choosing providers, while HMO plans prioritize managed care and cost containment. Medicaid plans provide coverage for low-income individuals but may have limitations in terms of provider availability and covered services. By comprehending these plan types, dental professionals can better navigate insurance processes. You can now decide for yourself what the different insurance types accepted at your future office will imply for you!

I will end this book with the long-promised bonuses chapter, chapter 13. This chapter will start by discussing some of the common expectations and realities you are likely to encounter when you start clinical practice, the contract terminology cheat sheet, Red Flags document, listed Learning Moments, the resume template and works cited.

Chapter Summary Points:

1. Similarities:

    a. **Basic Coverage: All three types of plans typically cover basic dental services such as cleanings, fillings, and X-rays.**

    b. **Managed Care: HMO and PPO plans both operate as managed care plans, meaning they have a network of dentists from which to choose.**

2. Differences:

    a. **PPO (Preferred Provider Organization):**

        i. **Flexibility: Patients have the flexibility to see any dentist, but they save money by choosing a dentist within the PPO network.**

        ii. **Out-of-Pocket Costs: Typically, patients pay more for out-of-network care.**

        iii. **Referrals: No referrals are required to see a specialist.**

    b. **HMO (Health Maintenance Organization):**

        i. **In-Network Requirement: Patients must typically choose a primary dentist within the HMO network and obtain referrals to see specialists.**

        ii. **Costs: Generally, costs are lower, but there is less flexibility in choosing providers.**

        iii. **Coverage Limitations: HMO plans may have more restrictions on covered services and providers.**

    c. **Medicaid-Based Dental Insurance:**

i. **Eligibility: Medicaid is a federal and state program that provides health coverage for people with low income, and its dental coverage varies by state.**

ii. **Coverage: Coverage can be limited, with a focus on essential services for children and sometimes limited coverage for adults.**

iii. **Provider Network: Dentists who accept Medicaid may be limited, and waiting times for appointments can be longer.**

3. **The Educated Associate can consider working for a FFS or PPO office to decrease the work burden while earning the same amount.**

Chapter 13

Bonuses

I wanted to round out the book with a bonuses section. This section is truly just that, bonuses that I wanted to include in the body of the text but simply ran out of space. Here you will find a section that talks about expectations vs reality, the long-promised Contract Terminology Cheat Sheet, the Red Flags Document, a summarizing list of the Learning Moments (LM), and a resume template for your usage. Wow that in itself is something others are charging $50 or more for and it's here as bonuses in an already greatly discounted book.

We will start with a section that discusses expectations and the reality that many associates would benefit knowing about before starting work. There are many things we as dental students think will be a reality, but when we get out into the workforce, we find many of those things are a lot less true than we had once hoped. Let's go through a few examples one by one.

1. <u>Expectation:</u> "I'm ready to do anything and everything."

<u>Reality:</u> You are a safe beginner. Dental school makes us safe beginners at best, but we certainly aren't trained at graduation to take on everything. It takes years, CE courses, and many hours of trial and error to learn new skills. To think we can do it all initially is ego inflating. Realize that referrals to specialists can be one of your best lifelines when starting work. As time goes on with practice, you can become proficient in many different surgeries, but it will take years beyond dental school to get there. I'm not even close to that point in my career. We can always grow!

2. <u>Expectation:</u> "I will be rich instantly."

<u>Reality:</u> You will earn better income than you are accustomed to, but it is exceedingly unlikely you will be rich right away. Most dental school graduates carry student loan burdens in excess of $300,000, they are in their 30s, and they are unlikely to have investments like real estate. We are at graduation *way* behind our same-aged peers who started their careers at 22 years old. Even though your income is likely to pass those peers alluded to above, we are still a long way behind in the game of finances. Learn to budget, reduce debt, invest, and grow your dental practice. My next big project will dive into these exact topics! I also provide one-on-one coaching on these very topics so when you are ready to be your own financial advisor, go to my website at TheEducatedAssociate.com and book a free call with yours truly. More on this topic below.

3. <u>Expectation:</u> "I need a financial advisor."

<u>Reality:</u> Many financial advisors operate on a fee schedule based on your assets under management that will reoccur every single year you use them. Some advisors charge 1% of your total assets, while others may charge a higher 2% fee. While these percentages may seem low, it's important to understand the actual impact on your finances. Opting for a financial advisor with a 2% fee can significantly affect the long-term account balances of a dentist. These fees gradually erode investment returns, diminishing the overall growth of the account.

For instance, if a dentist has a $1 million investment account and pays a 2% fee each year, they would be spending $20,000 in fees annually. Over 30 years, this could accumulate to hundreds of thousands of dollars that could have been invested in your portfolio and allowed to grow if the account was managed independently.

Financial advisors are typically engaged to assist in setting up accounts, providing guidance, and offering support during market fluctuations. While their services can be valuable for some individuals, it's crucial to evaluate whether the fees justify the services rendered, particularly for recent graduates with limited assets to manage.

Instead of allocating a substantial amount in fees to a financial advisor over their dental career, dentists can empower themselves by gaining proficiency in managing their finances. By educating themselves on financial principles and practices, they can make well-informed decisions and secure their financial future for the long term.

As mentioned above, my upcoming project will delve into financial education tailored for dentists, enabling them to learn how to handle debt, establish retirement accounts, and automate transfers to foster wealth accumulation over time. Equipped with the necessary knowledge and tools, individuals can take charge of their financial journey and potentially avoid the necessity of a financial advisor, especially in the early stages of their careers.

4. <u>Expectation:</u> "I need to buy a home."

<u>Reality:</u> Buying a home can be a wonderful step, and I know that it feels like we are behind our same-aged and non-doctor friends. There is certainly pressure to get that dentist house. I would caution you about jumping into more debt upon graduation, especially if you financed all of your dental education. You likely already have $300,000 or more in student loans; adding another $400,000-$1,000,000 for a mortgage can cause a lot of sleepless nights. Ask me how I know! I bought a house for $422,000 almost immediately after graduating and starting to work. We never missed or were late on payments, but there sure was a lot of our income tethered to debt between my student loan payment and the mortgage, which totaled over $3,300 a month at that point. I would encourage you to rent initially. This allows you to see if the

job is a good fit before digging any roots. Additionally, should the job not be a good fit, you sure don't want to have to sell a house you just bought for a potential move. If I could do my first year out of school over again, I would rent a house, save a 20% typical down payment, and have an emergency fund of several thousand dollars built up. That would make a home purchase much more feasible in year two at the same job!

5.   <u>Expectation:</u> "All patients will love me."

<u>Reality:</u> You are a great doctor and person. You will jive great with the vast majority of people you encounter in practice. There will, however, be a small subset that no matter how hard you try, they won't seem to like or appreciate you. I am a people pleaser, so this was really hard for me. In fact, it took me three years in practice to realize that I simply can't make everyone happy, and there are some people who won't be happy no matter what you do. When you find one of these people, don't stress over it, and try and move along from them as quickly as possible. I tend to refer these types of patients to specialists for literally anything and everything I can. Irreversible pulpitis on a #8, going to endo. Need a floating #29 extracted, go see the oral surgeon. It doesn't matter how "simple"—send those problem people out of your life!

6.   <u>Expectation:</u> "My schedule will be full daily."

<u>Reality:</u> It can take months or up to a year to build a true schedule. I have found that it takes at least one and more often than not two patient encounters for them to start trusting me. Since we meet most patients through hygiene exams and most patients are on six-month hygiene recalls, it can take a full year to have two encounters with the same patient. That means it might be a year before someone trusts you enough to schedule that filling with you. So be patient, keep doing your best work, but know a fully operational schedule won't be easy to develop until you have earned patient and staff trust.

7. <u>Expectation:</u> "I can have treatment times similar to those of the owning/mentor dentist."

<u>Reality:</u> The more seasoned doctor should be more efficient than you. If it takes the owner 1 hour to do three posterior resins and the office expects the same from you when you start, then you are setting yourself up for failure. The more seasoned dentist potentially has thousands of reps under their belt. You won't be as fast and it would be insane to think you will be. Be very realistic as you start when giving the scheduling team your estimated treatment times. Below you will see my recommended times for when I started.

    (i) <u>Posterior quad of resins:</u> 2 hours

    (ii) <u>Simple extraction:</u> 30 minutes

    (iii)   <u>Surgical extraction:</u> 1 hour

    (iv)   <u>Multiple extractions:</u> At least 2 hours

    (v) <u>Crown preparation:</u> 2.5 hours

    (vi)   <u>RCT (single canal):</u> 2 hours

8. <u>Expectation:</u> "I finished school—I am done learning."

<u>Reality:</u> Oh baby, the learning just started. Just a few years out of school, looking back at first year graduated dentist Dr. Schick, he was a total novice. We think we know a lot, and compared to how much we knew just a few years prior, we have grown, but in terms of knowing/being a master dentist, we are far from that at graduation. We really are safe starters as mentioned in part one above. Embrace learning as soon as you can wrap your mind around more learning. I know some graduates need a few months' breather from the rigors of dental education. Trust me, I understand, and if you need a few months to get settled and just be alive, please do that. At some point, however, your battery will be recharged and it's time to do some CE. As soon as you can, take

high-quality CE and keep taking it. The advances you will make at these courses will make you more profitable and able to treat wider and wider groups of patients. Always, select for learning over earning initially in your career!

9. <u>Expectation:</u> "I will be paid on simple production."

<u>Reality:</u> Very rarely are doctors compensated based on production alone. Office owners and corporations don't want to pay you when they aren't also getting paid—and hence pay adjustments. In the simplest sense adjustments are a fancy way of saying reductions to your pay for something the office didn't receive payment for. These can come from insurance adjustments, tax-write offs, and more. Be sure to evaluate your compensation structure closely if you think you will be paid on simple production. Sometimes the wording "simple production" is used, but the description in the following paragraph describes adjusted-production compensation, and the wording "simple production" was used in the preceding paragraph and was only there to trick you. Read the description rather than relying on the wording "simple production," "adjusted-production," or "collections" to see how you will be paid.

Imposter Syndrome

Another very important thing worth discussing as you start your career is the concept of impostor syndrome. Transitioning from performing procedures under the guidance of an instructor to independently diagnosing and treating patients is a significant obstacle for many doctors, including myself. It is a common experience for recent graduates to feel like they do not belong, often referred to as impostor syndrome. This feeling of being an impostor is completely normal and is a testament to how much we care about our profession.

To overcome impostor syndrome, it is crucial to cultivate clinical confidence. The most effective way to build this confidence is through repetition. Seeking mentorship, attending hands-on workshops/CEs, and gradually expanding our clinical skills are all ways to strengthen our confidence. It is important to start with treatments you are comfortable with and gradually challenge yourself with more difficult cases. Each time we acquire a new skill, we peel back a layer of the impostor syndrome onion and develop the competence needed to practice with confidence.

It is essential to remember that confidence grows with experience and practice. As we continue to gain clinical experience, our confidence will also grow. Do not be discouraged by impostor syndrome use it as motivation to improve and become the best doctor you can be.

One Year After Signing

Always be negotiating. If you've proven yourself valuable in the clinic where you work, be sure to negotiate a new contract at every possible opportunity. Be wary of agreements that carry over if nothing is said on your end at the end of the original contract term. For example, some agreements state that if you don't state otherwise by X date the contract renews. If the first contract was for a two-year term and you forget to negotiate a new contract after the first year of the contract, you may be roped into another two years of contract. If you initially signed a one-year contract, then 10 months into that contract start negotiating an extension or a new deal.

Typically, things like the pay structure and vacation time are more or less set in stone. Negotiating something like a lab fee reduction, however, is advisable. You can now show what kind of money you're bringing to the clinic. If you initially signed a contract in which you cover 30% of lab fees, try to negotiate no more lab fees or at a minimum a reduction to 15%.

Another aspect to consider renegotiating is one-time bonuses. Again, consider aligning your goal of earning more to an office-wide goal like more Invisalign case starts. At this point the owner has seen how you work and can really assess your value to them as a provider and employee. If you did everything you said you would initially, then they should feel like you are a great person to keep around. You can leverage your presence by stating how recruiting a new dentist is likely to cost them at a minimum several thousand dollars and maybe some time without an associate to cover the clinic. The stress of having to find a new dentist is often enough to tilt the needle in your favor during this negotiation. If you like working there don't get too greedy, but I think adding one or two opportunities for one-time bonuses into the second contract is beneficial for both the owner and yourself.

Continuing Education (CE):

While you likely just got done with four years of intensive training, you are already behind other dentists who graduated before you. Not only are they years ahead of you in your career, but they have likely taken continuing education courses since their graduation and therefore advanced their clinical skills in many regards. To mitigate this discrepancy in skills, I encourage you to attend high-quality CE right after graduation and to maintain this passion throughout your dental career.

There are two main avenues you can utilize when doing CE. There are individualized courses and then there is the academy/pathway avenue. The individualized courses are just that: stand-alone lectures, events, meetings, summits, hands-on training, etc. They are meant to teach/address one or two problems only. For example, you might attend a hands-on course learning how to laterally augment the maxillary sinus for future implant surgery. The course would be maybe a day or two in length, and you would leave with a better understanding of the lateral window surgery. On the academy/pathway avenue, you would sign up for something like Spear or Dawson Academies, which can function more like mini residencies. You would possibly travel to several different locations for different courses, and it would last much longer than a day or two. Obviously, there is a cost difference between the individualized approach and the academies. Personally, I have attended mostly individualized courses, but my DSO has recently struck a deal with Spear Academy and I plan to really dig into their academy over the next six months or so.

So, at this time what I have most experience with is the individualized courses. I wanted to learn implants, so I spent several thousand dollars in my first year after graduating doing two different courses on implant surgeries. The second course was a Neodent Summit in Las Vegas, which my owning doctor paid for. After the courses I gained the confidence to place and restore my own single unit implants, and by the end of the second year in practice I had placed and restored more than 10 dental implants. Not only was I advancing my skills, but the money I earned placing those implants easily covered the cost of the CE courses and I was still very early in my implant journey.

Since this time, I have continued to hone my implant surgical skills by taking a course on implant overdentures, and now I routinely recommend tissue-supported and implant-retained implant mandibular dentures. This has been a huge boost to the finances of my personal practice. At the end of the day, the advanced procedures have the best bang for your buck, so learning them early in your career is advisable.

The sooner you learn what types of advanced dental procedures you want to provide to patients, the sooner you can sign up and attend high-quality CEs to obtain those skill sets. CE is mandated by state boards but should be something The Educated Associate leans on to advance their skill set, thus allowing them to earn more. I want to leave you with an adage I love: "Early in our careers we should optimize for learning over earning."

Nowadays, while working at the associateship of my choosing, I often receive emails from offices I previously interviewed with or sometimes even offices I've never personally dealt with asking me to come in for a job offer. Here's a sentence pulled from a recent email and sent by an office I never interviewed with or even applied to: "We're very motivated to discuss terms and can make it appealing for you." The owner wanted me to call him that day to discuss contract terms. I'd never so much as sent him my email address. Nonetheless, from what he'd heard about me around town, I was the person he needed to solve his problem, so I could have set the terms of the contract. If you follow my plan (outlined in this book) and practice your negotiation skills, you'll soon find yourself in your dream associateship and turning down similar blank-check offers.

I wish you the best in your search for your dream associateship. I know if you spend the time and energy using the principles found in this book, you will find a job you love. I would love to hear more from you on what you thought about the book or how your search went or is going. I am available for phone consultation, which can be booked through my website, TheEducatedAssociate.com. Please leave a review on Amazon or wherever you ordered the book so I can continue to produce material that is helpful to dentists. Thank you for your time reading the book. The remainder of the pages holds the Contract Terminology Cheat Sheet, Red Flags, Learning Moments (LMs), templates you could use for a résumé, and the works cited.

As always, stay drilling my friends!

Contract Terminology Cheat Sheet:

Do you remember being a D2 and hearing some of the D4's students talking about their contract offers while doing your simulation lab? Did they only mention their percent production or daily guarantee? Did one seem smugger than the others because they had found a 35% pay somewhere? Let me ask you one more question: Did anyone follow up with the person who found the "highest pay" and see how long they stayed at the first position?

If you're like me, you were mystified by the idea of finding your dream job. The dream job, however, isn't just a direct deposit every 2–4 weeks. The dream job—and therefore the dream contract—is multifaceted and has many layers. Let's pull back some of those layers.

From an overview, there are typically 12-15 basic sections in an associate's contract. Here's a very simple overview to help you get through the sometimes nearly 20+ pages of legal jargon. Things noted in italics are intended to draw special attention so you can avoid a possible pitfall.

1. Introduction - Witnesseth/Recitals

    a. Who the parties are

    b. Why the parties are contracting together

2. Definitions

    a. Self-explanatory

3. Exclusivity

    a. Be cautious of restrictions on practicing elsewhere.

    b. If you wish to moonlight, volunteer, or do teledentistry, ensure written permission.

        i. Remember to formerly document any agreements to avoid conflicts.

            1. *Consider getting an addendum in your agreement or remove the exclusivity clause entirely to practice elsewhere.*

4. Term/Start Date

    a. When the relationship is expected to start

    b. How long the relationship is supposed to last

5. Schedule and Hours

    a. When and how often they expect you to work

6. Facilities

    a. Clarify where you'll practice and what resources you'll have.

    b. Ensure your agreement specifies the locations you'll bill for dental work.

    c. Be clear on facilities, equipment, and staff provided at these sites to avoid any confusion.

        i.   *If the owner has more than one location, ensure you will only work at locations you plan to bill at yourself!*

7. Duties

    a. Basically, so long as it doesn't entail breaking any laws, you'll practice dentistry the way the owner wants you to.

        i.   Owner decides what materials

        ii.   Owner decides which patients you see

        iii.   Owner can run the office the way they see fit and you can't criticize them for it

            1. *In a DSO practice, look out for a clause about referring all possible cases to specialists. The DSO may be seeking an internal referral to one of their specialists for up-billing.*

8. Compensation

a. How you'll be paid initially

b. Your normal compensation formula

   i.   *Net production = collections*

c. Possible formula for lab-fee deductions

d. How you'll be paid after giving notice (you'll likely be paid differently on the way out)

9. Benefits

a. Sick or vacation pay is unlikely

b. Other benefits are often hidden in the employee handbook.

   i.   Could change at the owner's discretion, any time for any reason

      1.   *If you have something important to you, get those specific benefits noted within the actual contract*

c. Malpractice insurance

   i.   Normally runs ~$150/month = $1,600/year

10. Termination:

a. Employer and employee notice requirements.

b. Termination by the employer can occur without cause → requires a specific amount of advance notice.

   i.   Amount of notice required for termination by employer is often shorter than time required for employee to give notice to the employer.

   ii.   Notice requires a proof of date, ie in writing.

   iii.   Termination for cause is often with obvious and inarguable lapses on the employee's part.

c. If employee doesn't provide sufficient notice → monetary punishment for each day you are short (most contracts will make you pay the company $500/day)

d. Some contracts will ask that you give them 90 days' notice but only require they give you 10 days' notice

   i. *Make sure the lengths of time match up*

11. Confidentiality:

    a. Return all printed and electronic information when leaving.

       i. Some DSOs have a two-week onboarding process, and they expect that information to be confidential and returned upon leaving the DSO.

          1. Watch the *Frontline* documentary *Kool Smiles.*

12. Noncompete agreements:

    a. *Negotiate time frame first and then radius*

13. Dispute Resolution

    a. Damages

       i. Important legal section regarding liquidated damages

          1. Both parties agree in advance that the terms of the deal are "reasonable."

             a. This way, if you ever try to sue them on certain grounds, the case will be thrown out.

          2. *Be sure to fully understand your exit strategy before signing the agreement.*

          3. Strike this clause if at all possible

    b. Non-solicitation of patients = no stealing patients

c. Non-solicitation of employees = no stealing the office's staff

d. Use of Name: Consider ownership and usage rights. If your name is important to you, get it in your contract that they have 3 months after you leave the associateship to remove your name from all marketing materials and the website.

e. <u>Assignability:</u> Assurance of personal responsibility for the work (you won't hire someone to fill in for you)

14. Governing Law:

a. The actual state in which you'd have to settle legal disputes

b. Entire Agreement: This is the only agreement and anything verbal isn't binding.

15. Signatures and Date

a. Now its official since you both signed!

Now you have a basic understanding of what should be in your agreement and an understanding of some common contract pitfalls to avoid so you should feel more prepared when reading your first contract. Next, I will lay out my exact strategy for reviewing an associate agreement so that nothing is ever missed.

<u>How to read an Associate Agreement:</u>

Contracts typically don't read front to back like a novel. Instead, they read in sections and sometimes the next section to read is three pages forward in the physical text. To make this easier, have a printed out and electronic version of the agreement available. Read the paper version and use the electronic to search for sections and subsections. I suggest a multi pass approach with a different focus on each pass through the agreement to ensure nothing is missed. At a minimum I would suggest every associate read their agreement at least once to make sure it's something worth considering before seeking outside advice. Below you will find my strategy for each pass through the agreement.

<u>First Pass Through the Agreement:</u>

- Gain a basic understanding of what is offered in a general sense

- Identify any major discrepancies between the offer and what was expected

- Determine if the offer is significantly different from what was discussed during the interview

  - ➢ Decide whether to proceed or decline based on initial impressions before delving into details

<u>Second Pass Through the Agreement:</u>

- Focus on the financial aspects of the agreement

- Review payment schedules, infirmity clauses, disclaimers, indemnification clauses

- Evaluate benefits offered based on personal needs and priorities

- Audit the agreement against personal benefit requirements

<u>Third Pass Through the Agreement:</u>

- Examine duties, expectations, and legal components

- Review scope of work, clinical responsibilities, patient load distribution

- Understand productivity expectations, schedule, on-call duties, vacation time

- Scrutinize termination clauses, notice periods, grounds for contract termination

- Check for malpractice insurance, liability, noncompete clauses, dispute resolution, confidentiality provisions

<u>Fourth Pass Through the Agreement:</u>

- Focus on nuances and questions identified in earlier passes

- Clarify any lingering concerns or areas of confusion

- Seek mentorship, guidance, or legal advice for specific questions

- Ensure full understanding of every word in the contract to make informed decisions

- Approach legal counsel with specific queries to optimize cost-effectiveness and understanding of the contract.

At this point, you have a proven strategy for reviewing an associate agreement. Next, I will define some common terms used in associate contracts to hopefully expedite your ability to read the document.

<u>Basic contract definitions:</u>

    a. <u>Overhead</u>

        i. Any ongoing expense necessary to operate the dental practice not directly related to patient care. These costs are vital for running the business but do not directly generate revenue.

            1. Examples of overhead costs include rent/mortgage payments, utilities, insurance, office supplies, equipment maintenance and repair, marketing/advertising, as well as salaries and benefits for non-clinical staff.

        ii. Overhead expenses are often considered fixed and do not fluctuate with the number of patients or services provided.

   iii.   Monitoring overhead closely is crucial for dental practice owners to ensure profitability.

b. <u>Revenue</u>

   iv. Total amount of money generated by a business from all its operations.

   v. The formula for revenue is (cost of service or good) x (# of units sold).

   vi. Revenue is typically reported on the income statement.

c. <u>Gross Earnings (GE)</u>

   vii. The revenue remaining after deducting the cost of goods/services sold (COGS), which includes direct costs associated with producing or delivering goods or services.

   viii. GE does not include deductions for operating expenses like salaries, rent, utilities, and taxes.

   ix. Most companies use GE to gauge their ability to generate revenue and cover direct costs.

   x. GE is also reported on the income statement.

d. <u>Net Earnings/Income/Profit (NE)</u>

   xi. The revenue a company earns after deducting all operating expenses, interest expenses, taxes, and other costs associated with doing business.

   xii. NE represents the total money left after paying all required expenses.

   xiii. Shareholders use NE to evaluate a company's profitability.

e. <u>Adjusted Production</u>

xiv. Refers to the dentist's gross production adjusted for factors like discounts, write-offs, or contractual allowances.

xv. Understanding adjusted production is vital for associate dentists as it influences their compensation or bonuses within the practice.

f. <u>Collections</u>

xvi. The actual amount of money received by the dental practice for services provided by the associate dentist.

xvii. Collections directly impact the associate's compensation, especially if their pay is percentage-based.

g. <u>Draw</u>

xviii. A predetermined amount paid regularly to the associate dentist, serving as an advance against future earnings or production.

xix. The draw provides a guaranteed minimum income, ensuring a consistent flow of earnings regardless of collections or production.

1. Note that deficiencies between the draw and collected amounts may result in penalties.

h. <u>Fee-for-Service (FFS)</u>

xx. Payment model where the dentist receives payment directly from the patient for services rendered, distinct from insurance-based or managed care arrangements.

i. <u>Insurance Claim</u>

xxi. A formal request submitted by the dental practice to an insurance company seeking payment for services provided to patients covered by the insurance plan.

j. <u>Indemnification</u>: This is legal obligation of one party (the indemnitor) to compensate another party (the indemnitee) for any losses, damages, or expenses that may arise in a specific situation.

1. Legal obligation to compensate for losses.

2. A way to allocate risk

   a. The indemnitor agrees to take on the responsibility of any losses or damages that may occur

   b. Clauses can become very complex and should be reviewed and negotiated with caution. Consider legal advice if you are confused.

At this point, you have a firm understanding of an associate agreement and can read the document without getting bogged down by the sections or terms in the sections. I want to ensure you don't get caught by any of the common red flags I have seen in associate agreements. So next, I will unveil the most common red flags I have seen in these agreements.

<u>Red Flags in Associate Dentist Agreements</u>

1. <u>Exclusivity Clause:</u>

   a. Watch out for restrictions on providing dental services elsewhere.

b. If you want to moonlight, volunteer or lecture, get an addendum stating that in your agreement or strike this clause outright.

2. <u>Facilities and Resources:</u>

    a. Ensure clarity on provided facilities, equipment, and resources.

    b. If the owner has more than one site, ensure your agreement only has you working at locations you plan to bill at yourself.

3. <u>Duties and Terms:</u>

    a. Pay attention to role outlines and ensure health-related provisions are fair and reasonable.

4. <u>Employment Scope and Schedule:</u>

    a. Define your scope of work, term, schedule, and leave policies clearly.

    b. Ambiguity in these areas could lead to misunderstandings or disputes in the future.

5. <u>At-Will Contracts:</u>

    a. Understand implications of termination rights.

    b. Consider how this may affect your flexibility and security in the position especially in relation to signing bonuses.

6. <u>Readability and Accessibility:</u>

    a. Ensure the contract is clear and easily understandable.

7. <u>Legal Review:</u>

    a. Consider seeking legal counsel for complex terms or anything you don't fully understand.

Dr. Schick's Opinion on Legal Review:

While I never personally used an attorney for contract review, seeking legal counsel is recommended, especially if there are complex or unclear terms in the agreement. Legal advice can help ensure that your rights and interests are protected. If there is ever a slight concern that you don't fully understand the agreement, get legal help next!

By being aware of these potential red flags and points of concern, you can approach the review of an associate dentist agreement more critically and proactively address any issues that may arise. As a final way to evaluate the agreement I wanted to provide a way to synthesize the compensation/ benefits offered between offices and therefore directly decide which agreement is more valuable to you.

Evaluating your Total Compensation:

This is a formula to help determine how much your benefits boost your actual income. This calculation provides a comprehensive view of your entire offer, combining both compensation and benefits. For instance, in some university settings, although the salary may appear low, the benefits could account for over 20% of your total salary, unlike most private practices. This calculation allows you to more directly compare offers in terms of total compensation.

Total Compensation Value Formula = Base Salary + Value of Benefits

To calculate the value different benefits add to your compensation package, a dentist can use the following equation:

<u>Base Salary:</u> The dentist's annual base salary amount. Determine what your normal monthly income will be and multiply by 12.

<u>Value of Benefits:</u> The total value of various benefits provided in the compensation package. See list below for ballpark estimates.

Begin by assigning a monetary value to each benefit in the package, such as healthcare coverage, dental insurance, retirement contributions, continuing education stipends, and other perks. Consider industry standards and geography when estimating the values:

- <u>Healthcare Coverage:</u> $4,000 to $12,000 per year for single coverage. More for family.

- <u>Dental Insurance:</u> $200 to $600 per year

- <u>Retirement Contributions:</u> 3% to 6% of annual salary

- <u>Continuing Education Stipends:</u> $1,000 to $5,000 per year

- <u>Professional Memberships:</u> $500 to $1,000 per year

- <u>Malpractice Insurance:</u> $1,000 to $3,000 per year

These are general estimates, and actual values may vary based on the employer and benefits offered. By adding the base salary to the total value of benefits, the dentist can determine the overall compensation value, providing a comprehensive view of the financial worth of the offer. Then you can compare one offer to another in terms of total compensation.

By now, you understand your agreements and can compare the different agreements in terms of total compensation much more directly. Next, we will discuss the many Red Flags brought up in the body of the book.

<u>Red Flags in Dentistry:</u>

In this section of the chapter, I summarize the many red flags that were brought up throughout the book. This is meant to service as a quick reference sheet to make sure you don't fall victim to the many ploys out there to trick associate dentists.

1. <u>Office Reviews:</u>

a. Before applying, check Google for office reviews. Pay attention to how the office manager or owner responds to negative reviews.

    i. A responsive and constructive approach is a positive sign, while being combative or dismissive is a red flag.

    ii. Multiple recent negative reviews may indicate underlying issues.

    iii. Avoid places where the owner is hostile towards feedback.

2. <u>"Wearing Multiple Hats"</u>:

a. When an employer says they need someone who can "wear multiple hats," it often means they expect you to take on additional responsibilities beyond your main role of being a dentist without proper compensation for the added responsibilities.

b. Be wary of being overworked and underpaid.

3. <u>"We're Family"</u>:

a. This phrase may indicate a toxic work culture dominated by cliques.

b. Be cautious as you might be pressured to attend numerous "non-mandatory" events that feel obligatory.

4. <u>"We pay our associates on collections so they can learn to do the most important thing in dentistry—make the patient pay"</u>:

a. If the job pays associates based on collections to push them to ensure patient payments, it could suggest poor financial practices within the office.

b. Watch out for a lack of support from the Office Manager in collecting payments from patients as the responsibility of collecting is unfairly shifted to associates.

c. I would run from owners that make comments like this to you.

5. <u>Interview-Agreement Alignment:</u>

a. Taking notes of proposed compensation and benefits during interviews to compare with the contract terms can help ensure transparency and honesty from the owner.

b. Misalignments between promises made during interviews and the contract terms should be considered red flags.

6. <u>Collections-Based Pay:</u>

a. Many owners justify using collections-based associate pay by saying "it aligns the associate's interests with those of the practice since both parties benefit from increased collections."

b. I've also heard owners say things like, "It teaches young doctors the most important aspect of owning a business, which is to collect the money."

i. Question the rationale behind collections-based associate pay, especially if it is justified as aligning interests between the associate and the practice.

ii. Quite literally associates are there to do dentistry and the office is there to provide support. Associates should not be burdened with responsibilities that should be handled by the owner.

    1. Associates wanting to produce more should always be your goal.

    2. Offices wanting to collect 100% of everything produced should be their goal.

c. Production based contracts directly align these goals.

d. Collections contracts aren't automatic deal breakers. Just watch out for comments around collections within these contracts.

7. <u>New Patient Practices:</u>

a. Ensure fair distribution of new patients and avoid arrangements where the associate receives limited opportunities.

b. You should get access to at least your portion.

    i. If it is a two-doctor office, you should get half of the new patients.

    ii. If it's a three-doctor office, then you should get 33% of the new patients.

    iii. So on and so forth.

8. <u>Success Timeline:</u>

a. Be cautious of owners setting unrealistic expectations of immediate success within a short timeframe, think 3 months or less.

b. Building trust with patients and establishing a successful practice often takes time, my experience has been at least 6 months.

    i. Aim for a reasonable guarantee pay period, such as 6-12 months, to allow for patient recognition and trust to develop.

9. <u>Facilities and Resources:</u>

    a. Review the facilities where you will be practicing and ensure that the necessary resources, including staff and supplies, are provided.

    b. Verify that only the offices you plan to bill at are listed on your specific agreement.

    c. I would strongly encourage you to make sure the following sentence is in any agreement you sign:

        i. "[XYZ employer] is responsible for providing the associate dentist all necessary equipment and appropriately licensed personnel to effectively complete their job as a dentist in [XYZ state(s)]."

10. <u>Duties Section:</u>

    a. In a DSO practice, be wary of clauses that require referring all cases to in-house specialists, as this could indicate a strategy for up-billing where you lose out on potential income.

    b. Pay attention to the tone of voice used in the educational materials provided by the employer.

By being aware of these red flags and carefully evaluating job descriptions, you can make informed decisions about potential employment opportunities in the dental field.

This next subset of red flags was never directly discussed in the text but was either vaguely referred to or something I felt was just too important to leave out but there just wasn't room in the body of the book for discussion, so I added it here.

1. <u>Unclear Compensation Structure:</u>

   a. Beware of vague or confusing compensation models that may not align with industry standards or undervalue your work.

2. <u>Excessive Noncompete Clauses</u>:

   a. Watch out for overly restrictive noncompete agreements that could limit your career options or geographical mobility post-employment.

      i. Consider negotiating shorter time frame first then radius secondarily.

3. <u>Lack of Mentorship Opportunities:</u>

   a. Ensure the practice offers adequate support and mentorship for your professional growth and development.

      i. If you go there for a year or two and don't learn any new skills, how will that make you feel?

4. <u>High Patient Turnover Rates</u>:

   a. Be cautious if the practice has a history of high patient turnover rates, as this may indicate underlying issues with patient satisfaction or quality of care.

   b. This can obviously impact your income.

5. <u>High Staff Turnover Rates:</u>

   a. When there is a revolving door of staff members something is almost always amiss.

      i. Maybe the owner or office manager has poor communication style, or the staff feels unsupported.

   b. Whatever the reason might be, significant staff turnover should be evaluated closely for the reason(s).

6. <u>Pressure to Over-Treat Patients:</u>

   a. Avoid practices that prioritize profit over patient well-being, leading to unnecessary or excessive treatment recommendations.

   b. Try and get a feel for this while your boots are on the ground at the in-person interview or office tour.

7. <u>Inadequate Continuing Education Support:</u>

   a. Practices that choose not to support the growth of their providers is a sign of bad corporation in my mind.

   b. If you aren't growing, you're dying.

8. <u>Limited Autonomy:</u>

   a. Be wary of practices that restrict your clinical autonomy or decision-making, hindering your ability to provide quality care.

      i. This can weigh heavily on your subconscious if you lack autonomy.

      ii. I would encourage you to run away from opportunities that will restrict your autonomy in any way.

9. <u>Financial Instability:</u>

   a. Research the financial health of the practice to avoid getting caught in a situation where financial issues could impact your job security or compensation.

10. <u>Poor Work-Life Balance:</u>

   a. Prioritize practices that promote a healthy work-life balance to prevent excessive stress or professional burnout.

Please use these red flags as a sort of litmus test to ensure the office you are considering signing with doesn't have something ominous lurking in the background that might sabotage the start to your dental career.

Next, we talk about the many Learning Moments (LMs) discussed throughout the book.

<u>Learning Moments:</u> Things to Lookout for & Tips for Avoiding Mistakes Myself or Other Colleagues made

1. <u>Avoiding Time-Wasting Job Applications:</u>

   a. When applying for jobs, it's crucial to focus on positions you genuinely want.

   b. Don't fall into the trap of applying to jobs you wouldn't consider accepting.

      i. If you know you won't work on kids, don't apply to an office that sees primarily pediatric patients.

2. <u>Understanding Contract Types:</u> Independent Contractor vs. Employee

   a. <u>Independent Contractor (IRS Form 1099):</u> Independent contractors are self-employed individuals responsible for their taxes and are not entitled to company benefits.

   b. <u>Employee (IRS Form W-2):</u> Employees receive benefits such as health insurance and retirement plans, with taxes withheld by the employer.

3. <u>Trusting Your Instincts:</u>

   a. Listen to your gut during the interview process to avoid potential issues like harassment or unhappiness in the workplace.

4. <u>Focus on Team Dynamics:</u>

a. When trying to decide if you will like a practice long term, the people in the practice end up being far more important than the specific setting whether that is Private Practice or DSO.

5. <u>Keeping Your Options Open:</u>

   a. Early in your career, having multiple job offers provides you with more opportunities for growth and development.

   b. Don't dismiss job opportunities prematurely without considering the benefits they may offer.

   c. Collecting contract offers early in your career:

      i. Builds confidence in your approach.

      ii. Provides practice in reviewing and negotiating contracts.

6. <u>Assessing Cultural Fit:</u>

   a. Observing how potential employers behave during interviews can offer insights into their management style and work environment.

   b. If you aren't certain consider offering a paid working interview so you can directly see how you and the owner will interact.

7. <u>Monitoring Performance Metrics:</u>

   a. Regularly track your production and billing numbers to ensure accuracy in claims and procedures.

      i. I pull up my production and collections numbers daily.

      ii. Address any billing discrepancies that day to avoid issues down the line.

8. <u>Understanding Collection Rates:</u>

    a. Analyze collection rates to have a clear picture of the financial aspects of the practice, 96% or higher tends to indicate healthy collecting principles.

        i. Obtain information about top insurance carriers. Especially fees associated with said carriers and the dental offices top three grossing dental procedures and their associated collections percentages with the previous associate.

    b. Be aware of how billing practices can impact your income as an associate.

9. <u>Financial Planning:</u>

    a. Prepare for fluctuations in income by creating a budget that accounts for variable pay periods.

        i. Be ready for large adjustments to future pay by understanding insurance.

    b. Planning ahead can help alleviate financial stress during uncertain times.

10. <u>Reviewing Contracts:</u>

    a. Thoroughly review and understand all aspects of your employment contracts before making decisions.

    b. Careful analysis will help you make informed choices about your career opportunities.

    c. Collections contracts aren't inherently bad, while simple-production contracts are not inherently good.

        i. Every contract can be good or bad. You must review it to decide for yourself.

11. <u>Exclusivity clauses in contracts:</u>

a. Determine if you can practice elsewhere during the specified period, including moonlighting, volunteer work, lecture circuit or teledentistry.

   i. Obtain written permission for any additional work outside your primary employment to avoid conflicts.

b. Consider making changes to the agreement if you desire to perform pro bono work and/ or attending charitable events.

c. If you plan to "moon light" at other offices, move to strike this clause.

d. If you plan to lecture or offer education, also move to strike this clause.

e. Consider negotiating or adding an addendum to specify your desired flexibility.

12. <u>Non-Compete Clause:</u>

a. In multi office operations you need to clarify whether non-compete clauses apply to all office locations or only where you provide services.

   i. Ensure that any restrictions are limited to practices where you bill for services, as broad non-compete agreements can severely limit your future job prospects.

      1. This is especially important in large DSOs.

b. Negotiate a shorter time frame first then a shorter radius next.

   i. Aim for a noncompete period of no longer than 1 year, ideally 6 months.

13. <u>The Facilities subsection:</u>

a. Pay attention to specific addresses listed, especially in corporate settings.

   i. Strike any locations where you don't plan to actually bill dental services

14. <u>Resources subsection:</u>

    a. Ensure the necessary equipment and licensed personnel are provided in employment agreements.

    b. I would strongly encourage you to make sure the following sentence is in any agreement you sign:

       i. "[XYZ employer] is responsible for providing the associate dentist all necessary equipment and appropriately licensed personnel to effectively complete their job as a dentist in [XYZ state(s)]."

15. <u>Infirmity clauses in contracts:</u>

    a. You are signing an agreement to avoid becoming unable to work due to physical or mental health issues.

16. <u>Bonus type:</u>

    a. Understanding what type of bonus, the office plans to pay you is important.

    b. There are signing, relocation, starting and many more types of bonuses offices can leverage to get a dentist on staff.

       i. If you need the money to move across state to start your new job, then you need a relocation bonus that is paid well before your start date.

       ii. In one instance, my wife, a pediatrician, was promised a bonus of $15,000, which we thought was a relocation bonus. To our surprise, she received the bonus only after beginning work. Essentially, it turned out to be more of a starting bonus as opposed to a true relocation bonus. We had counted on having the funds for our move, which unfortunately was not the case.

c. Understand the type and when you will actually have the funds in your account to make sure you avoid the mistake described above.

17. <u>Benefits:</u>

a. Often benefits are listed in the Employee Handbook, which is up to change at any time, whereas your agreement is set in stone once signed.

b. Ensure that important benefits are explicitly outlined in your contract rather than solely relying on the employee handbook, which may be subject to change at the owner's discretion.

18. <u>Treating Friends and Family Members:</u>

a. If you plan to treat friends or family members, then you need to get it in writing what this will look like financially for you and the patients.

b. Some offices will allow for greatly reduced fees on family members while other offices won't offer a discount whatsoever.

19. <u>Termination:</u>

a. Verify that the notice periods required for termination align between you and your employer to avoid any discrepancies.

i. For instance, if your contract mandates a 90-day notice from you, ensure that the employer's notice period is equitable, such as 90 days as well.

b. I strongly suggest knowing your exit strategy before signing the contract

    i. Understand financials of leaving as well as possible future work restrictions

20. <u>Placing a Compensation Anchor:</u>

a. When negotiating your pay rate, consider positioning your anchor towards the higher end of the pay spectrum for your geographic region.

b. By setting an expectation of higher compensation, such as 32-35% adjusted production, you can influence the negotiation process positively.

c. This approach can significantly enhance your pay rate with minimal effort.

21. <u>Work-Life Balance:</u>

a. Remember to prioritize your mental health as an integral part of your work-life balance.

    i. Get a Hobby!

b. Engaging in activities that bring you joy, like bike rides, can have a profound impact on your well-being.

c. Taking care of yourself is essential to providing optimal care to your patients.

22. <u>Shadowing or assisting in your future office:</u>

    i. In some states obtaining your state license may take weeks to months following graduation.

    ii. Some offices will ask you to come in and shadow or assist during this waiting period.

    iii. While maybe a day or two the week before you start may help acquaint you to office supply locations acting in any role other than dentist sets up in a weird position. Trust me, Ive been there.

    iv. Additionally, you are a dentist and dentists should be compensated as dentists not assistants so tread lightly on the shadowing or assisting roles.

23. <u>Patient population and Provider burnout:</u>

    i. The primary patient population the office you choose to work at can affect your personal level of job satisfaction significantly.

    ii. Making sure you get the patient population right on a personal level can help stave off burnout.

24. <u>Home-Office Locations and Burnout:</u>

    i. Long distances between your residence and your place of work results in many unpaid hours commuting.

    ii. Shorten the distance if at all possible, to have more time at home as opposed to on the road.

25. <u>Personal Differentiator:</u>

    i. Use your personal statement to identify a unique characteristic about you or your dental practice.

    ii. Remember your unique attribute doesn't have to be a specific dental treatment or procedure and instead could be something less tangible, like my ability to calm anxious patients.

26. <u>Always ask, the worst they can say is "no":</u>

    i. Whenever there is a job or negotiation opportunity you should take it 100% of the time. The worst thing you can hear is "no".

    ii. Like Wayne Gretzky says "you miss 100% of the shots that you don't take."

27. <u>Paper Copies to Interview:</u>

    i. The act of bringing physical copies of the cover letter, CV and any certifications or licenses you have earned to an interview acts as a much stronger phycological lever than the list on the CV alone.

        1. Even if your pile would be the same as everyone else in your dental school class, the pile looks way better than a single piece of paper.

28. <u>Signed Agreements:</u>

    i. Your associate agreement needs to be signed by both you and the employer for it to carry any legal ramifications.

        1. A handshake deal means literally nothing.

29. <u>Upfront and Honest:</u>

    i. When interviewing I find it best to always be upfront and honest. If you have a pre-existing medical condition that might affect your work, let them know.

        1. If they respond poorly at least you found out in advance of starting work how they would respond.

30. <u>Clawbacks:</u>

    i. Be sure to evaluate the termination section of the agreement to assess for clawback provisions.

    ii. Clawbacks can be used against previously dispersed bonuses or benefits.

31. <u>Regional Clinical Board Exams:</u>

i. Just take and pass all five sections as a dental student even if your expected state of practice doesn't currently require all five sections.

32. <u>NPI:</u>

i. Never expires or renews.

ii. Just needs updated when your practice location changes.

33. <u>Reference List:</u>

i. While in dental school or away on rotations be sure to start creating a reference list of practicing dentists.

ii. Some states require character references who are dentists themselves.

34. <u>Occurrence-Based Coverage:</u>

i. This type of insurance covers any incident that occurs during the policy period, regardless of when a claim is filed.

1. Even if a claim is made after the policy has expired, the incident is still covered if it occurred during the policy period.

2. This type of coverage should be preferred by dentists (LM).

3. If your employer is planning to pay for your malpractice insurance but will only offer a claims-based policy, I would encourage you to negotiate the occurrence-based option into your contract or see if they will pay the cost of the claims-based policy toward an occurrence-based policy you set up for yourself.

35. <u>Insurance Credentialing:</u>

    i. The process where an insurance company ok's you to work on their signed up patients and for you to subsequently seek reimbursement for the treatments that you provide.

    ii. Can take weeks to months for full provider credentialing with some insurance carriers.

        1. Have your future office start credentialling you as soon as you sign the agreement.

When I read the list of LMs I'm always surprised how many things I had to learn first-hand, that hopefully by reading this book you will avoid. Please send me any LMs I may have missed through my website at TheEducatedAssociate.com so I can add them to future versions of the book and so you can help future doctors learn from you!

Please feel free to use the résumé template below to start your job application process!

Résumé Templates:

https://drive.google.com/drive/folders/1zYce0gQe0if3RHVRabbLH61Lq9Of3c1V?usp=sharing

Works Cited:

Bureau of Labor Statistics. "May 2020 Occupational Employment and Wage Statistics." U.S. Department of Labor.

American Dental Association (ADA). Official Website.

DentalPost. "2020 Annual Report." DentalPost.

Payscale. Official Website.

National Network of Oral Health Access (NNOHA). Official Website.

National Association of Dental Plans. Official Website.

Last Week Tonight with John Oliver. Season 8, Episode 15. HBO.

Parks and Recreation. Season 4, Episode 4. NBC.

Voss, Chris. Never Split the Difference: Negotiating As If Your Life Depended On It. HarperBusiness, 2016.

Chapter Summary Points:

1. Leverage the Contract Terminology Cheat Sheet to quickly review your agreements

2. Use the Learning Moments (LM) to avoid many pitfalls common to associate dentists

3. Review the Red Flags document to make sure there's nothing obviously wrong with the practice

4. Use the provided template to make a simple but AI readable resume.